EYESIGHT MANDALAS

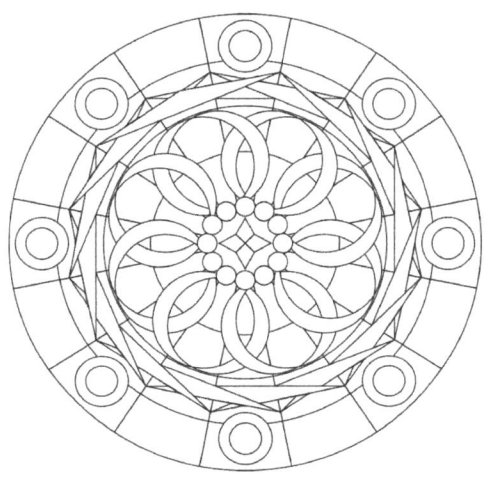

DEDICATION :

Dedicated to everyone who experiences eyesight strain and/or
muscle strain from intense coloring activity.

ISBN-13: 978-1522775218

ISBN-10:1522775218

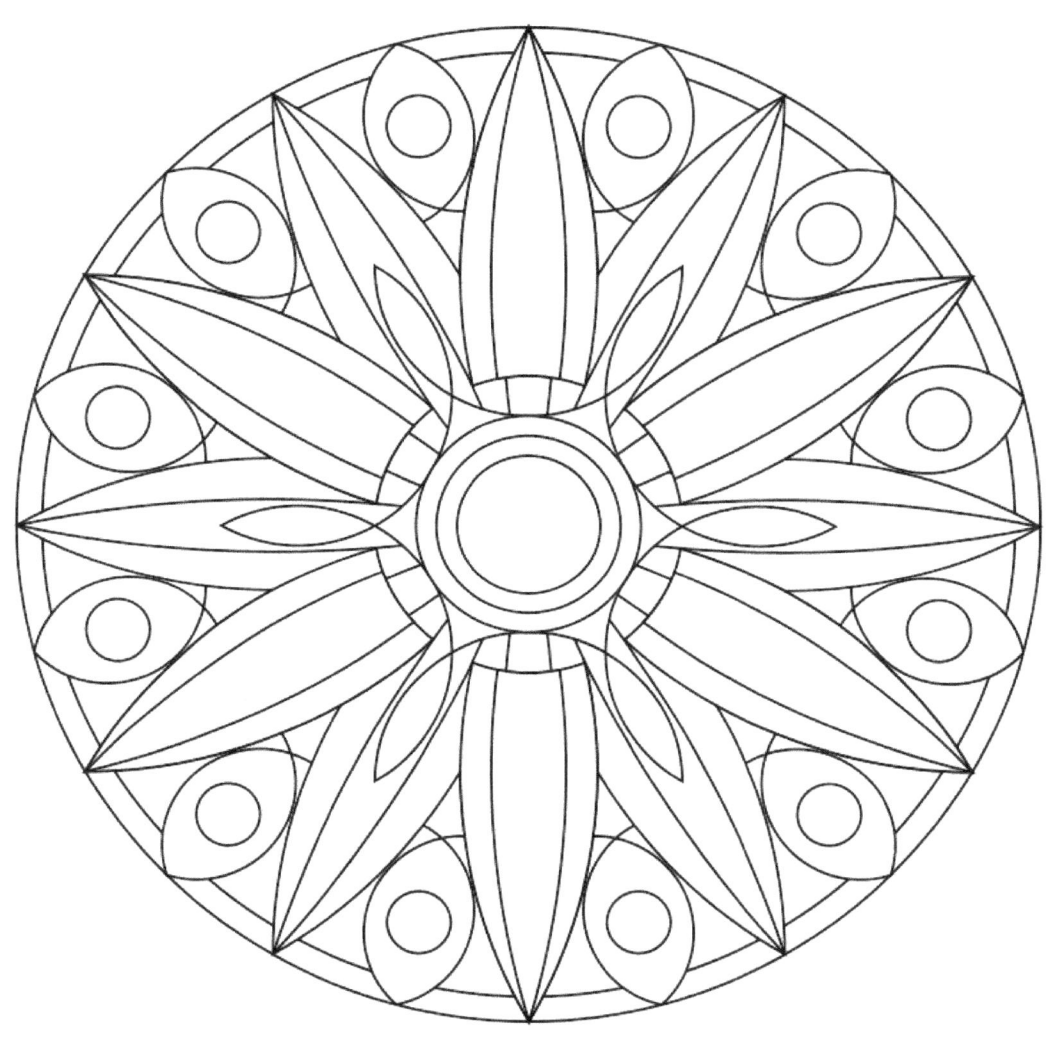

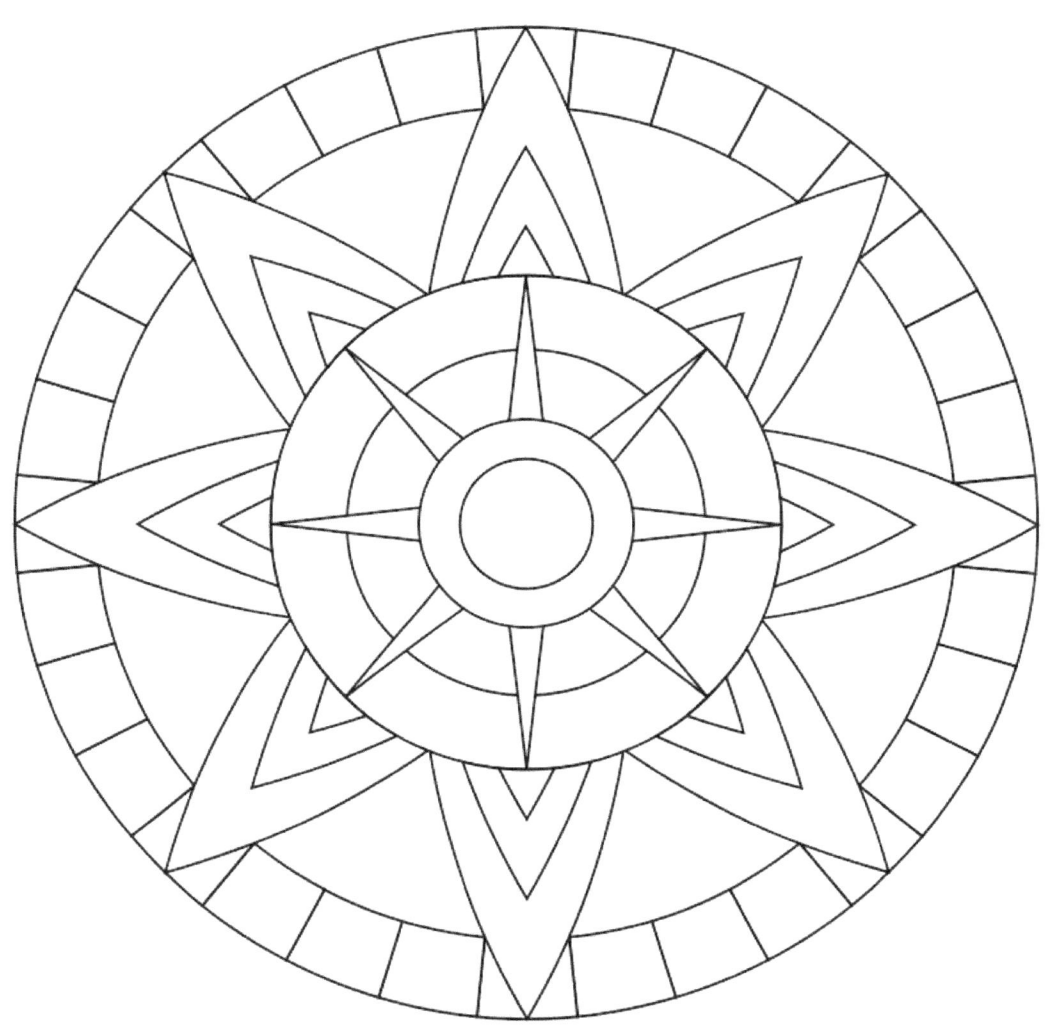

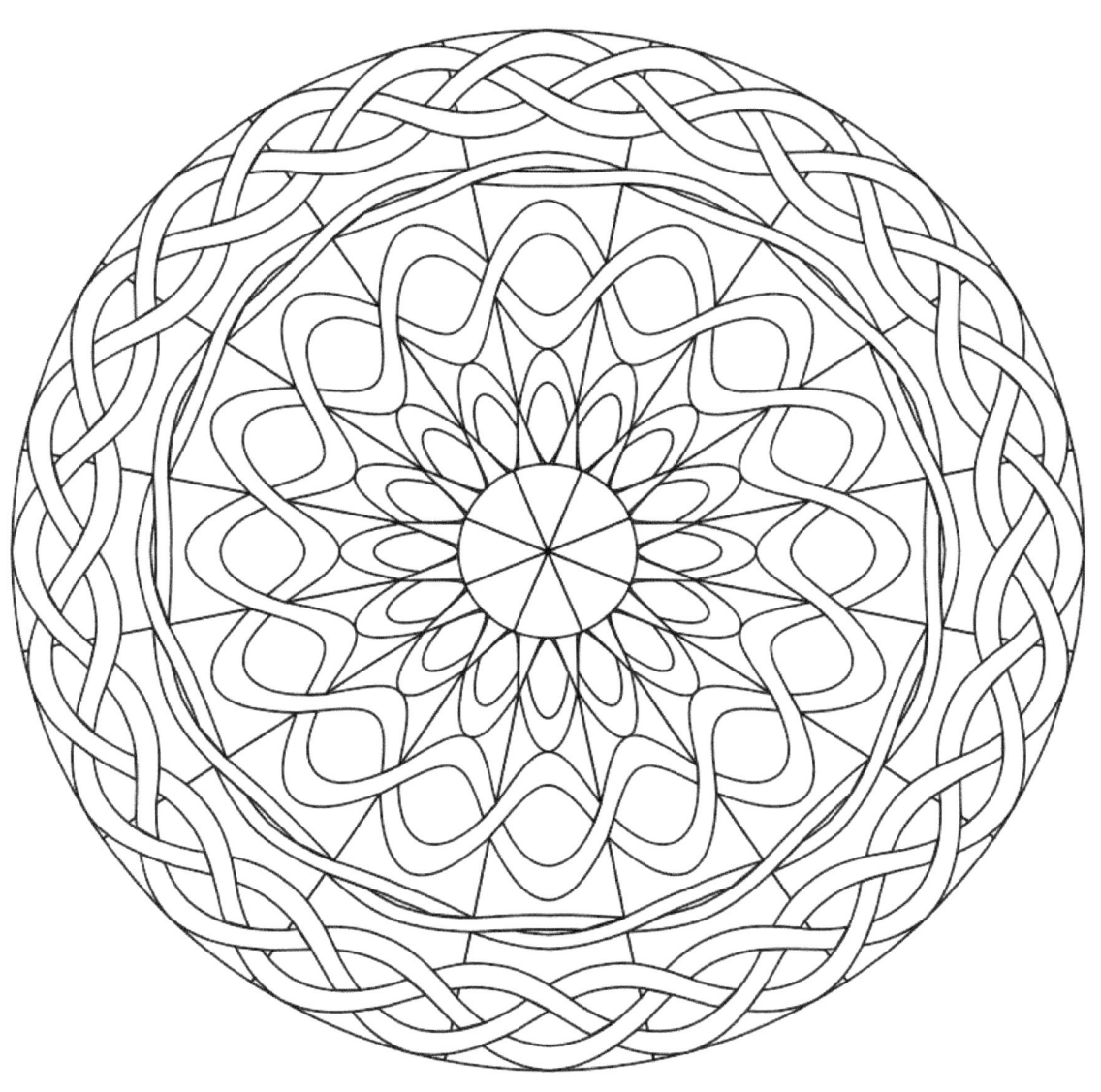

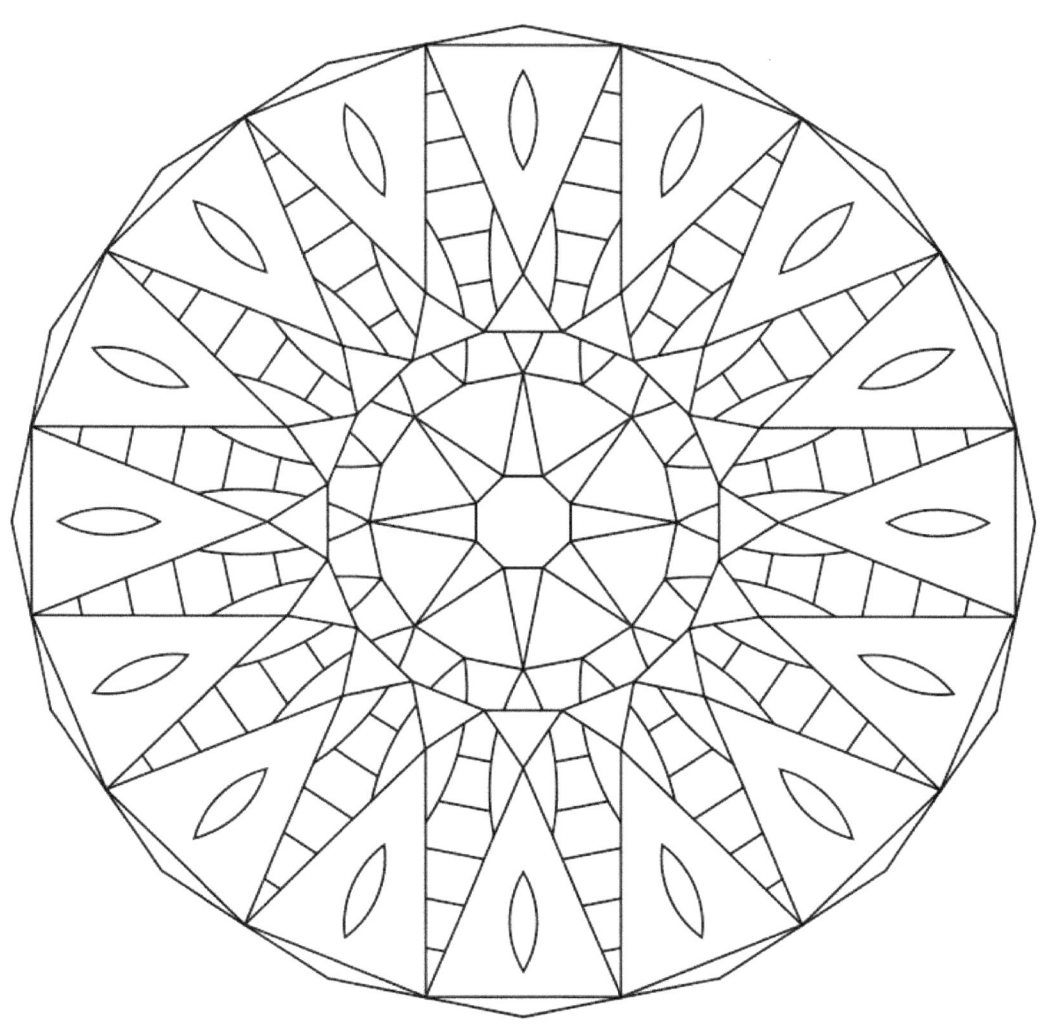

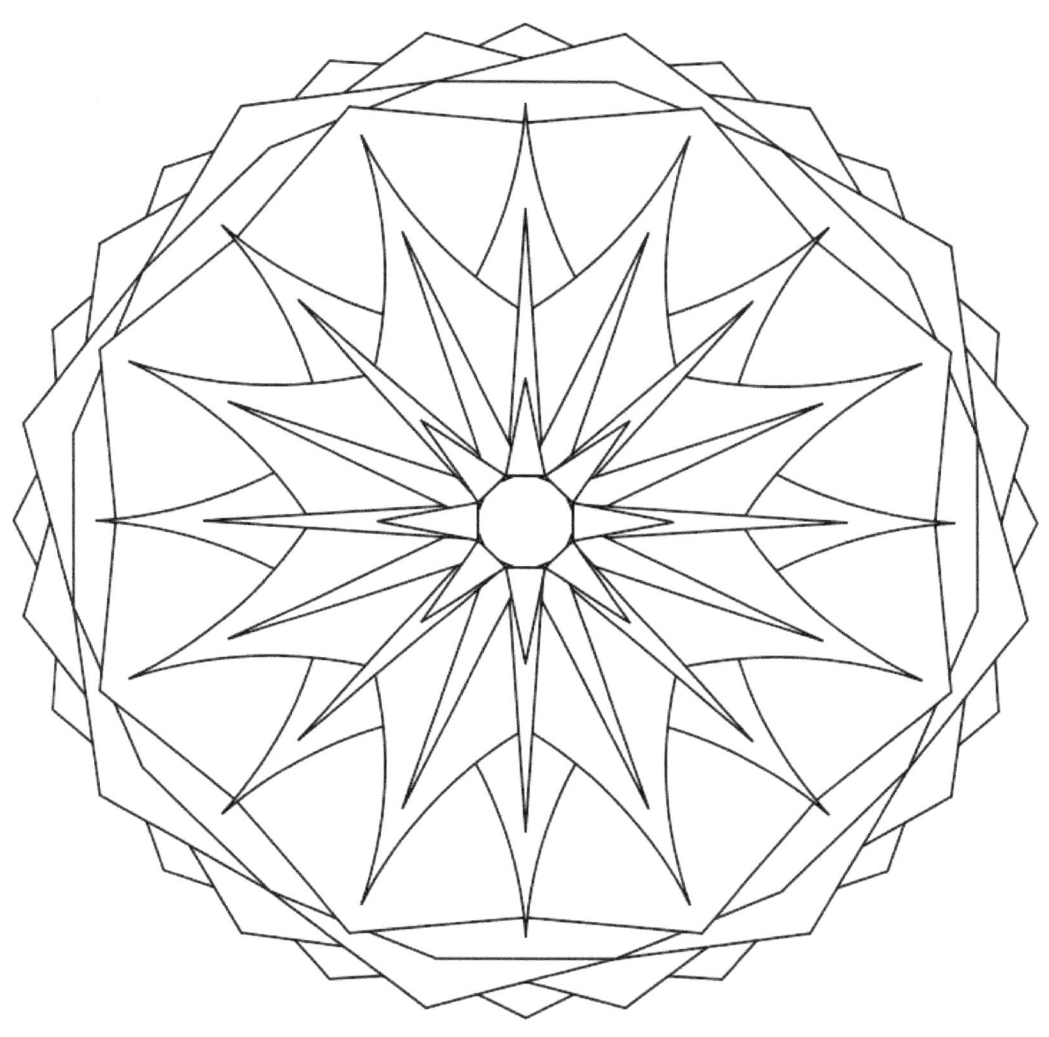

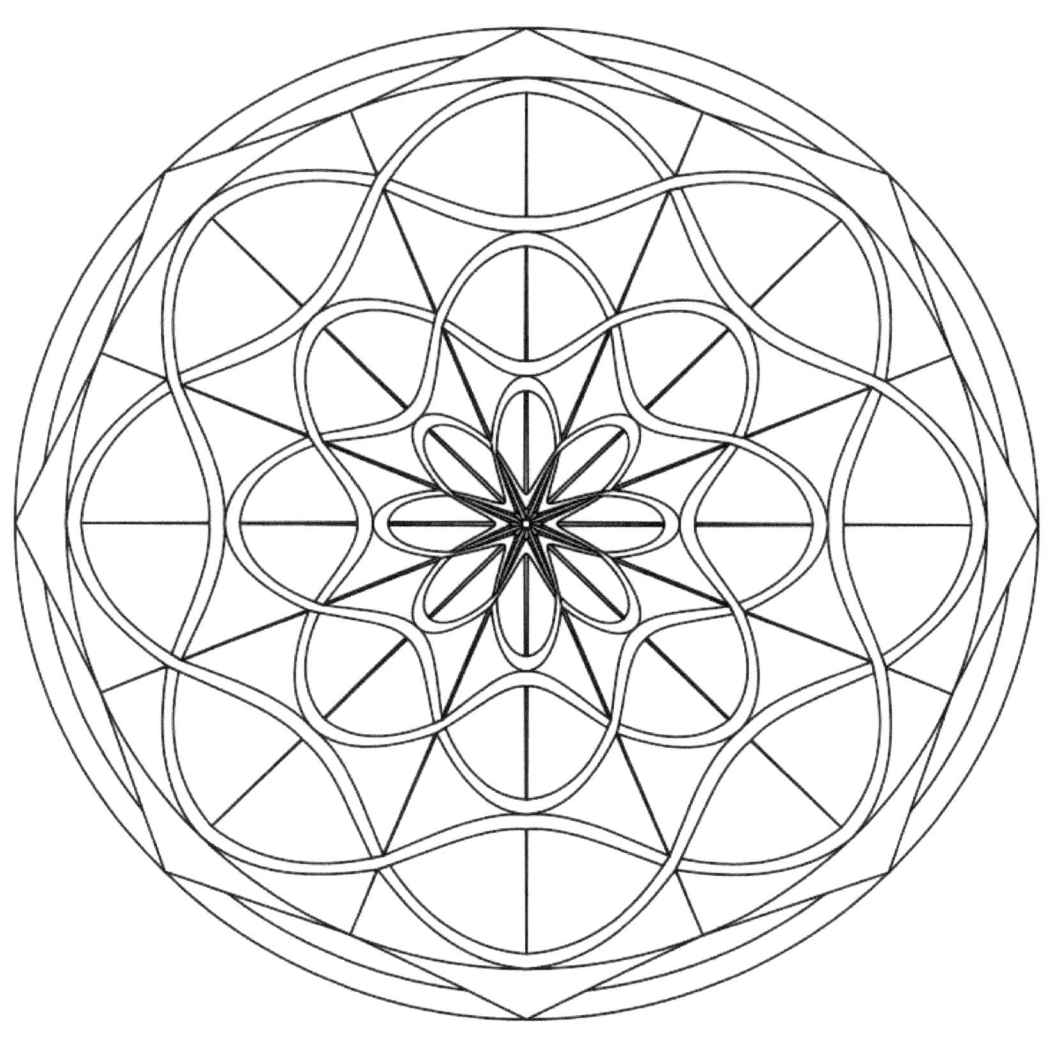

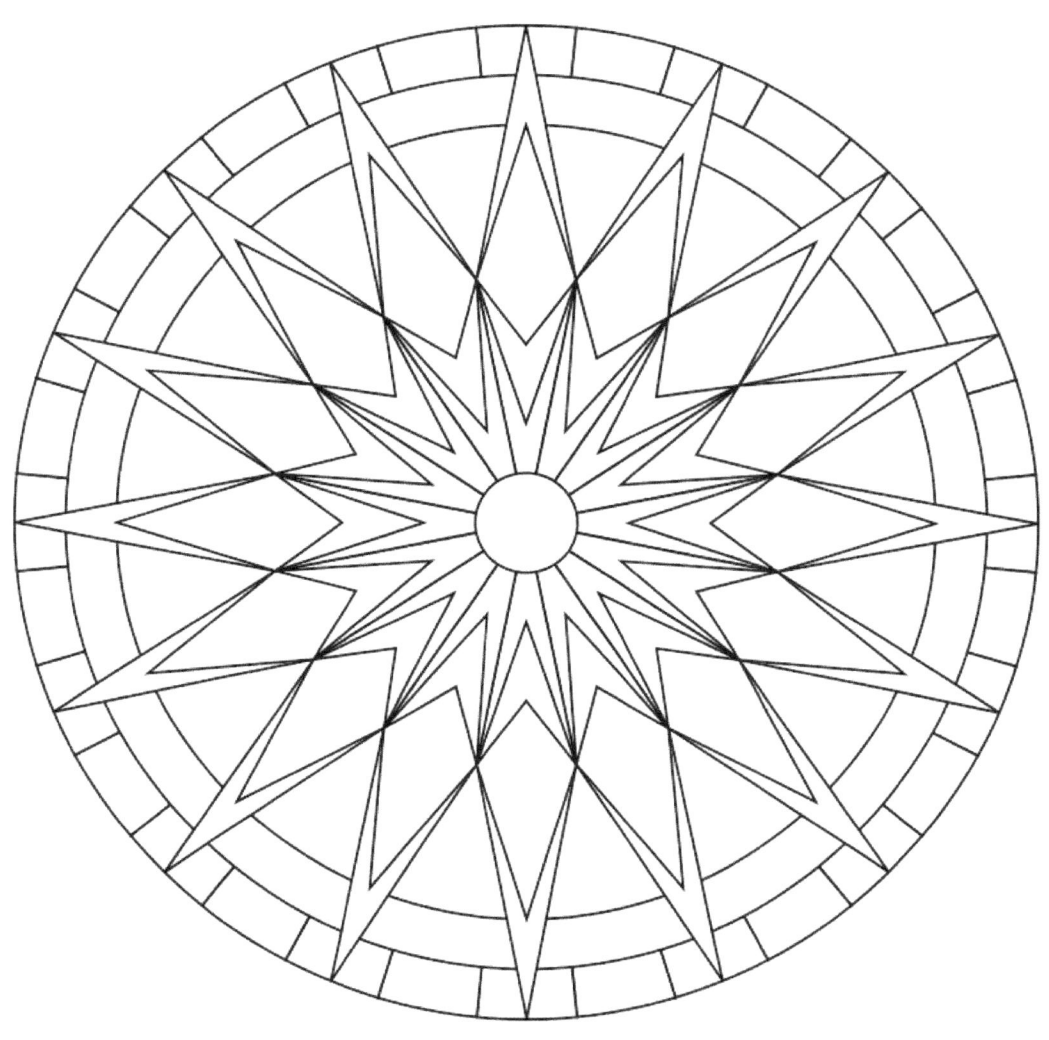

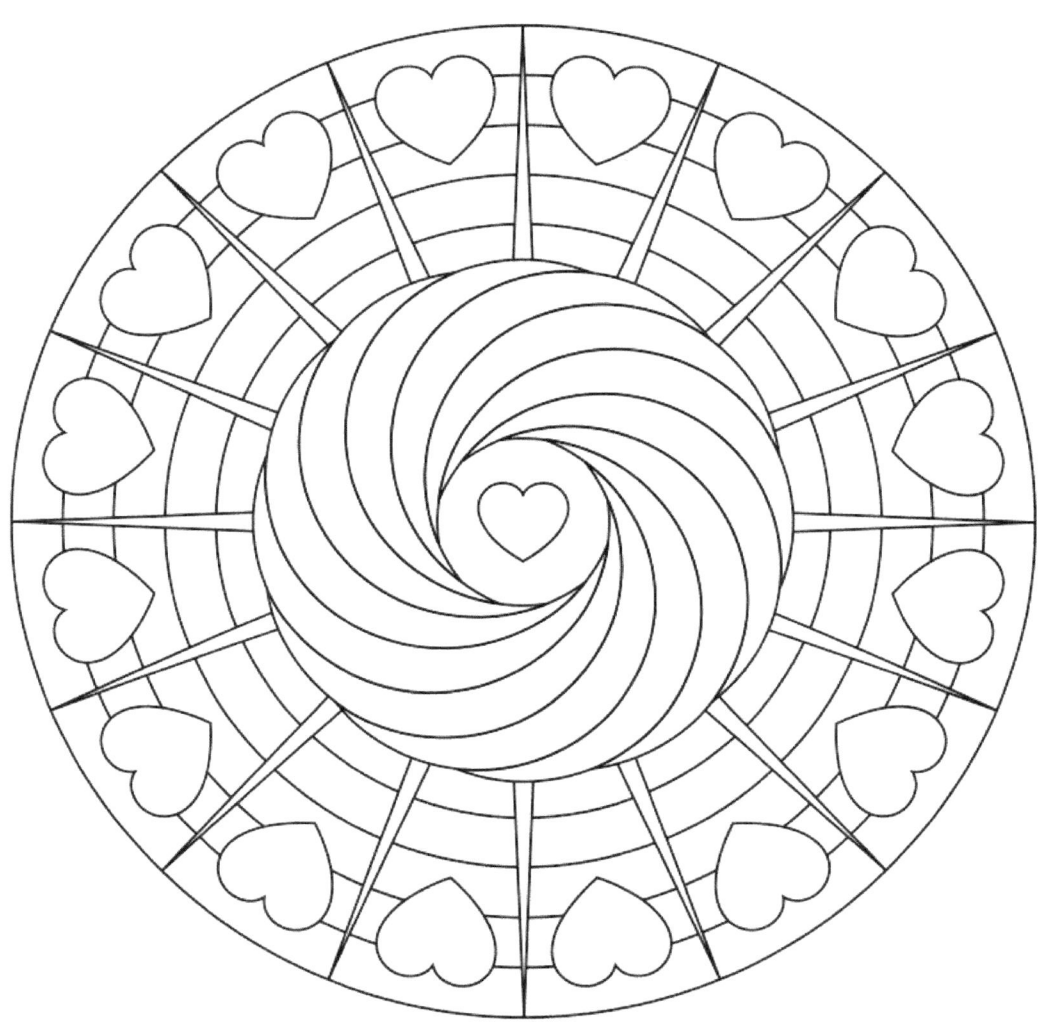

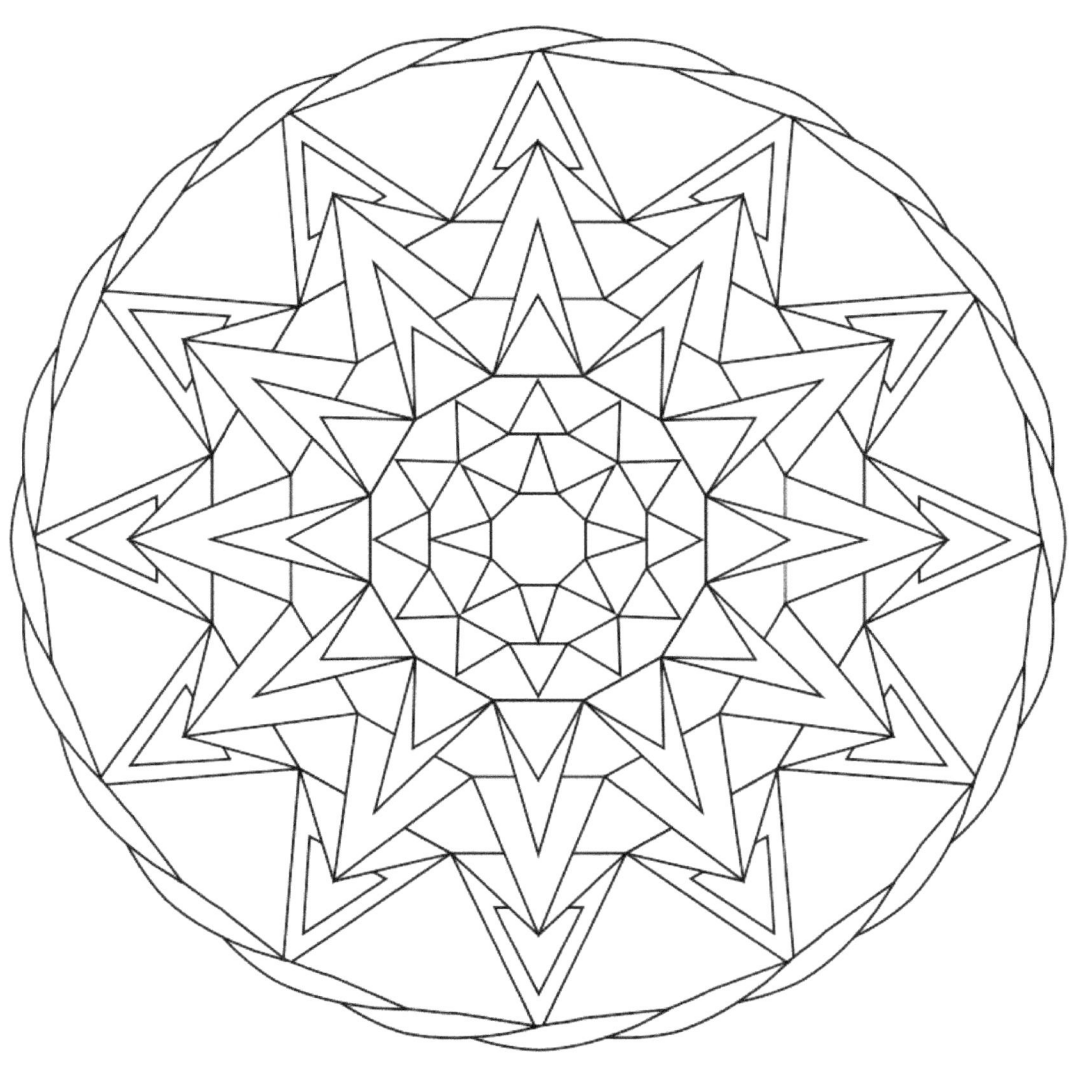

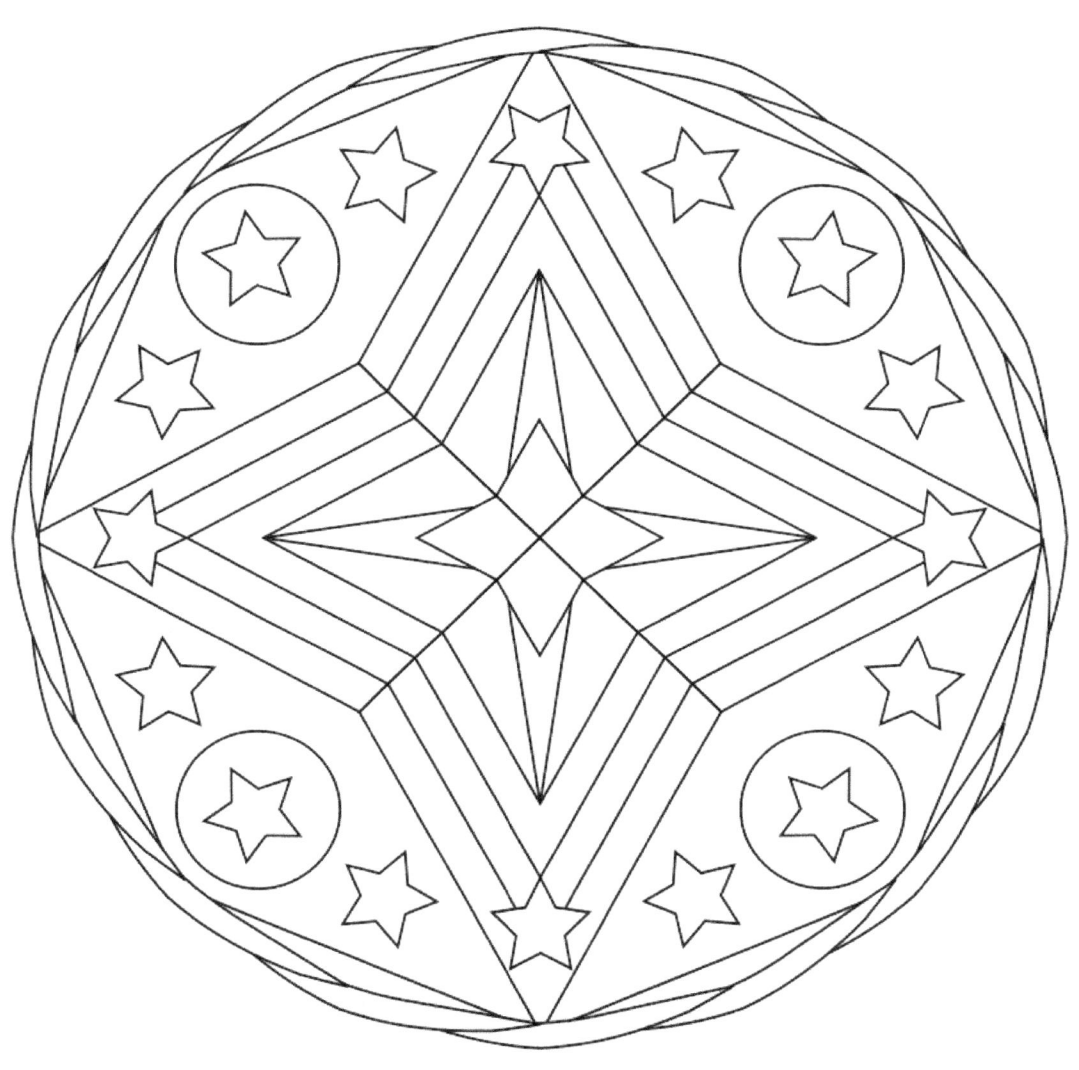

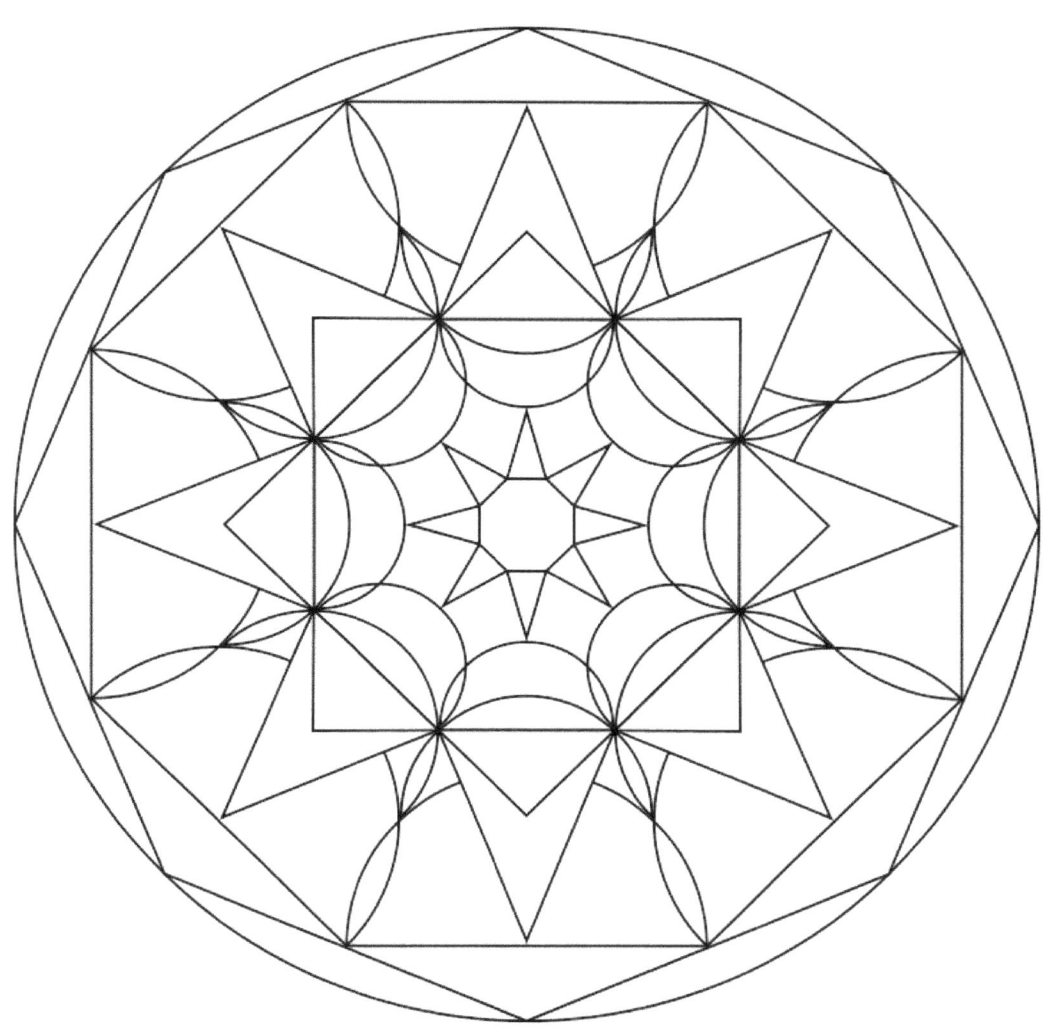

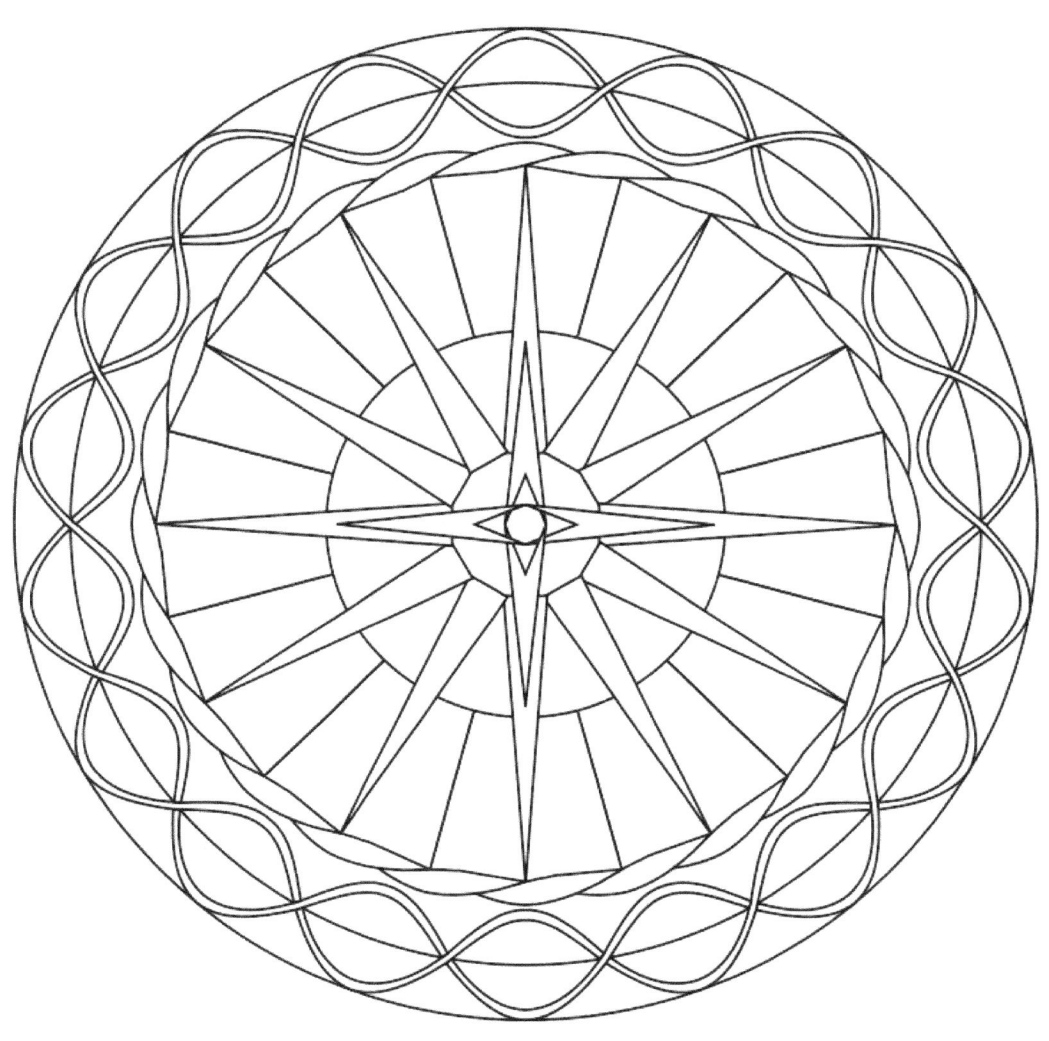

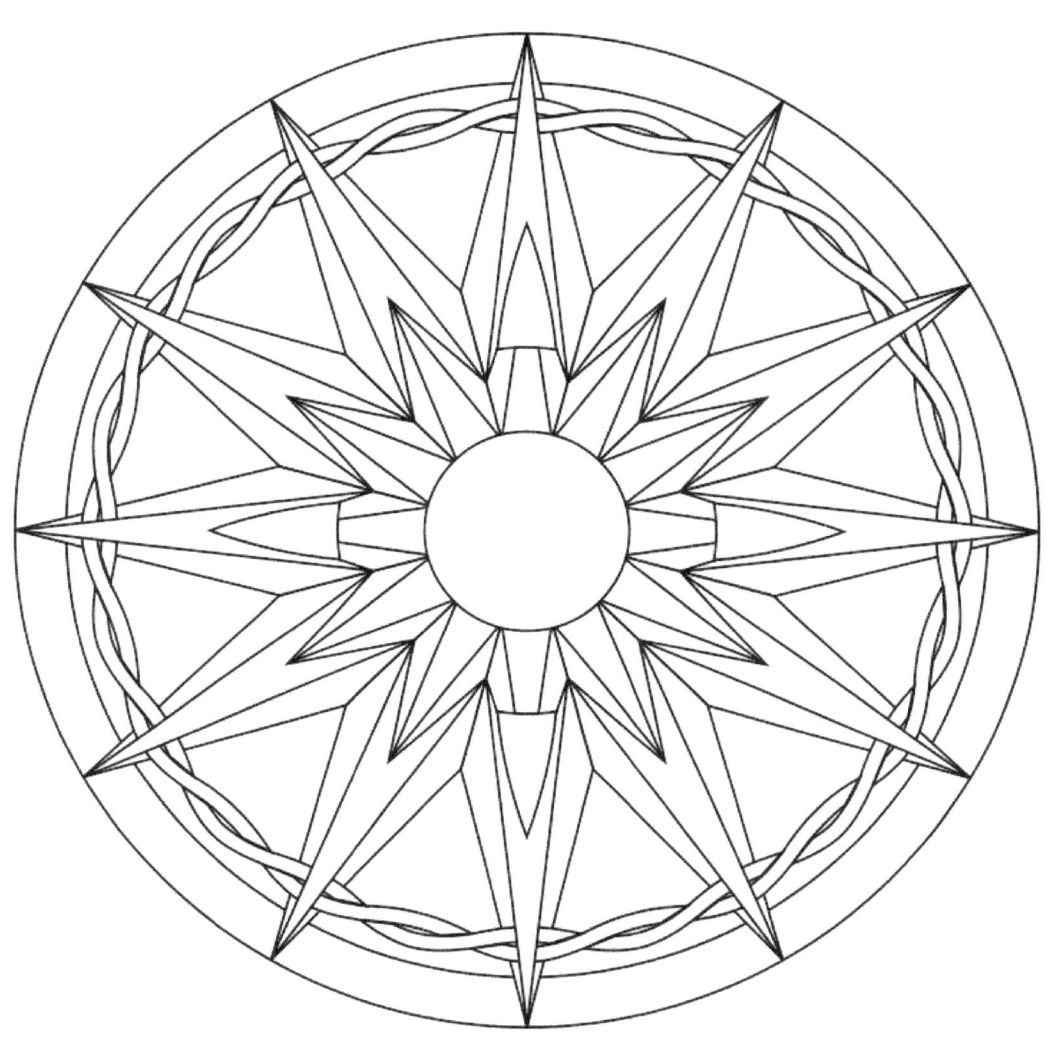

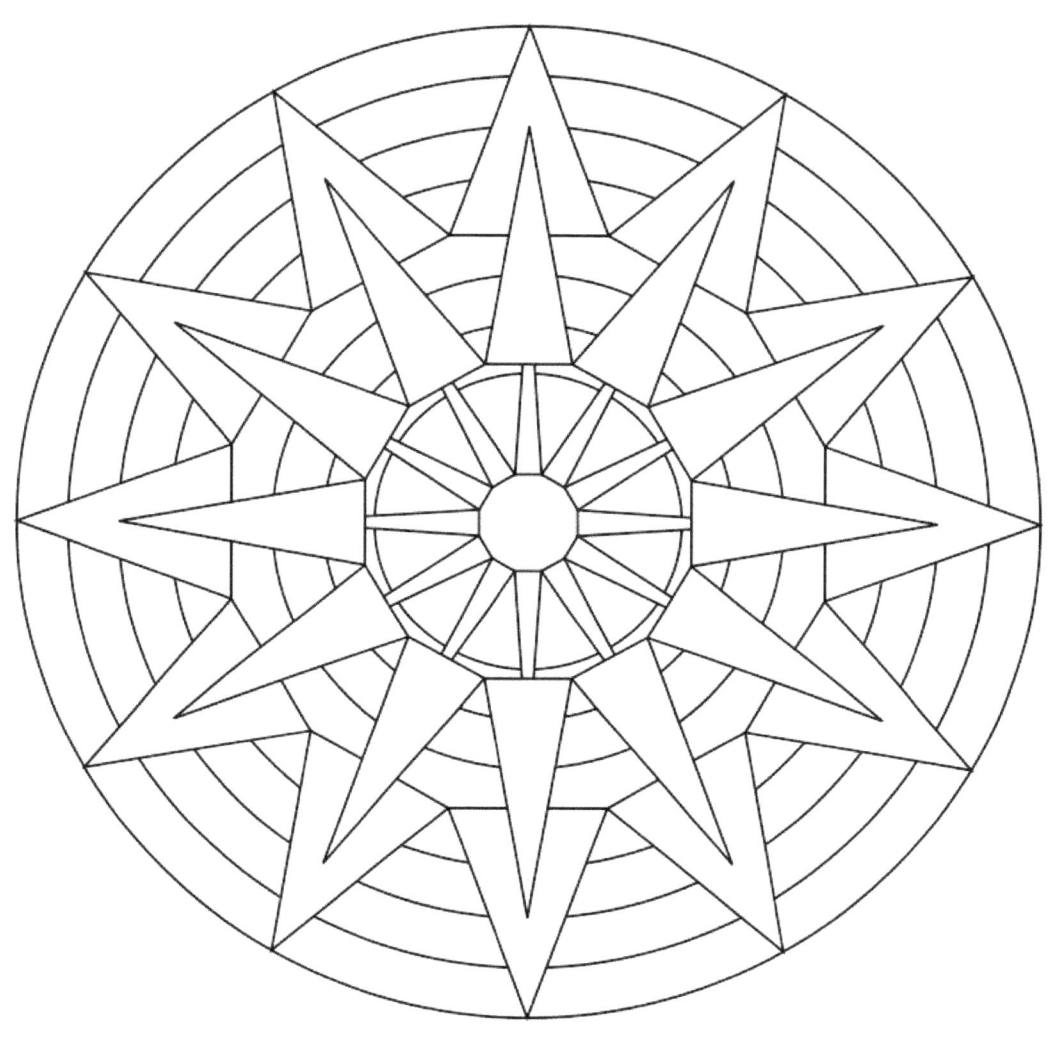

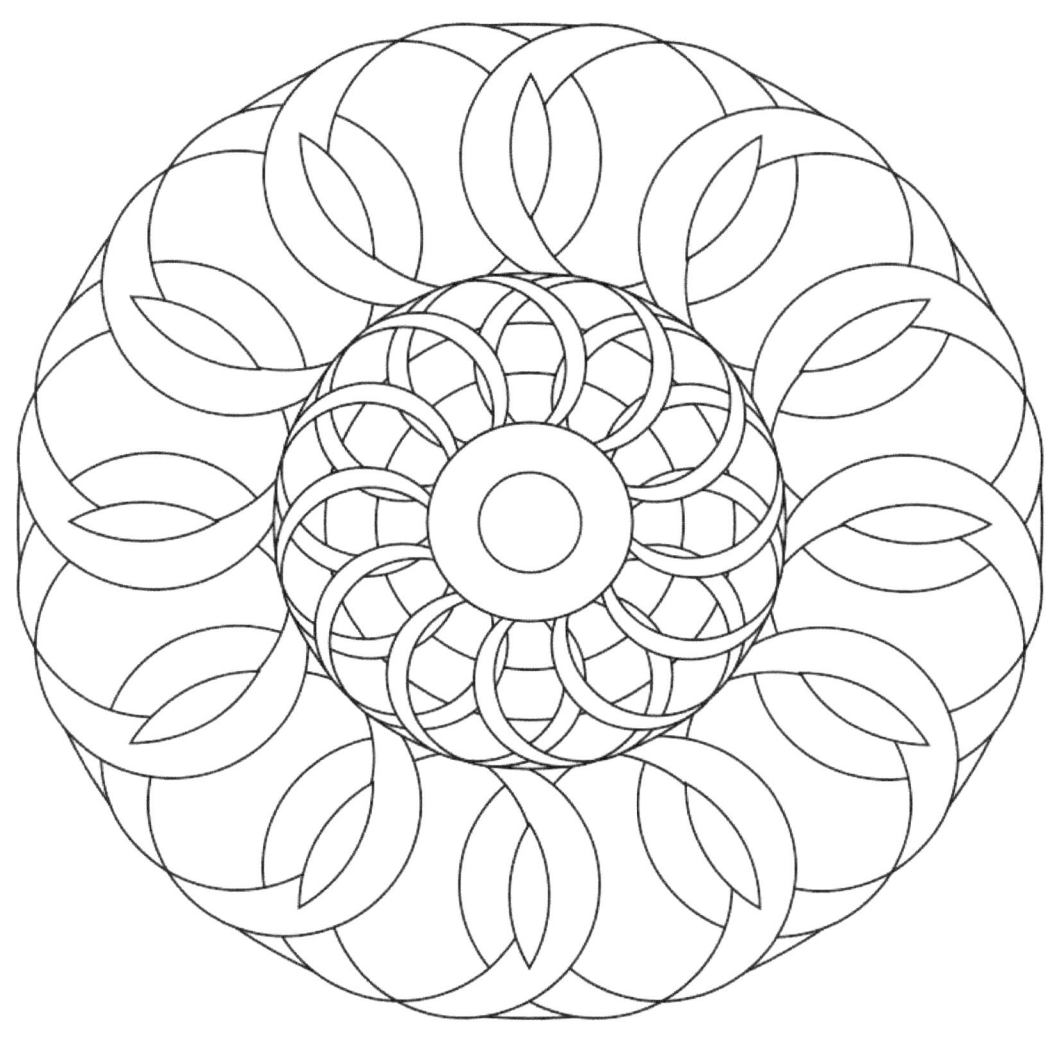

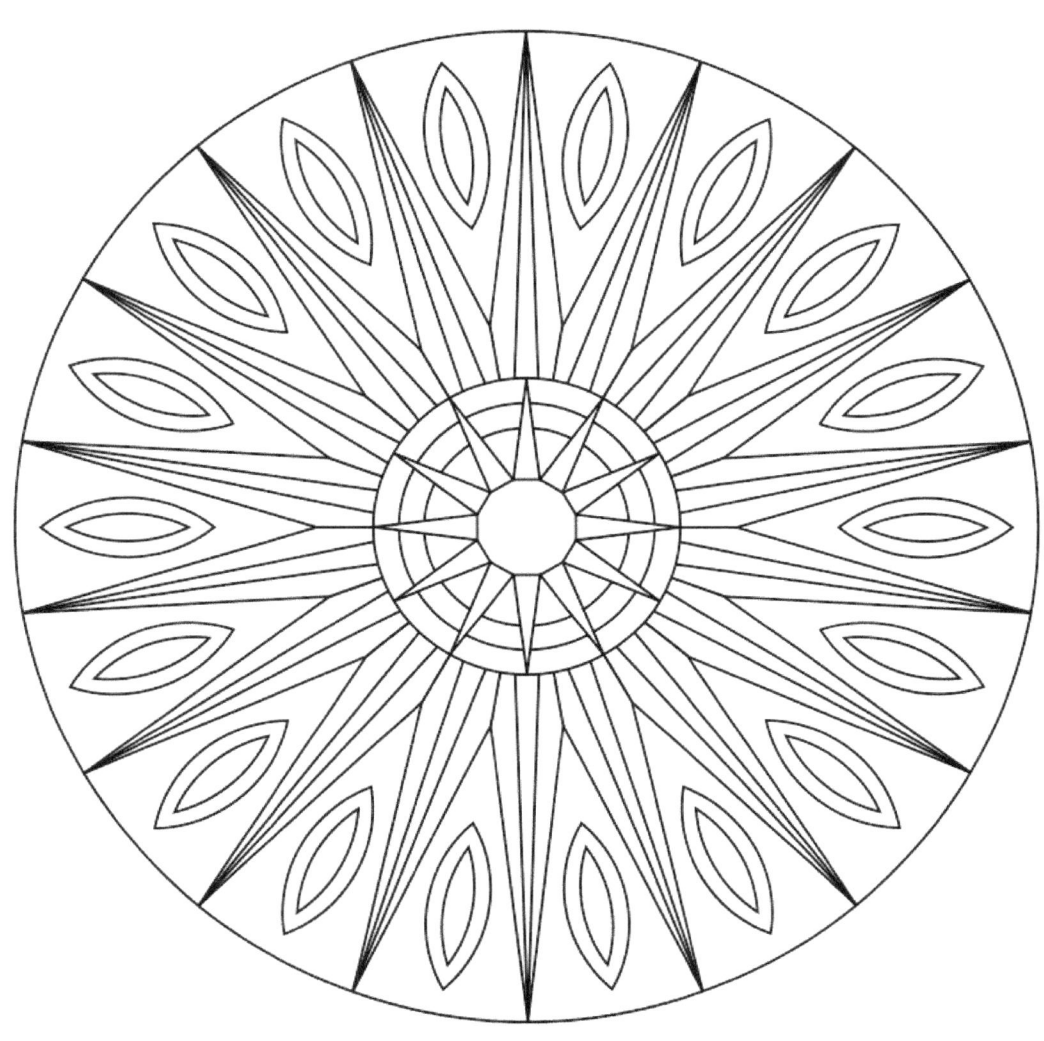

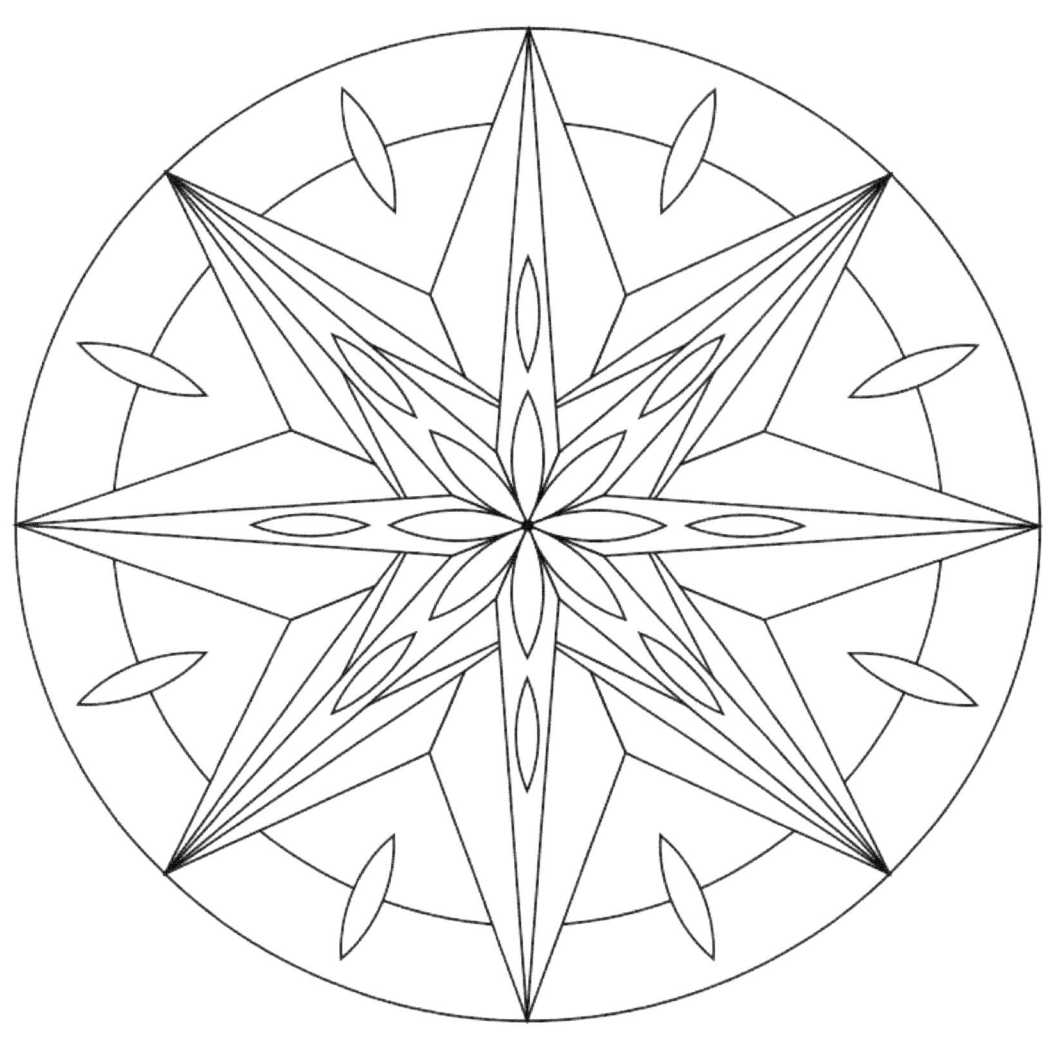

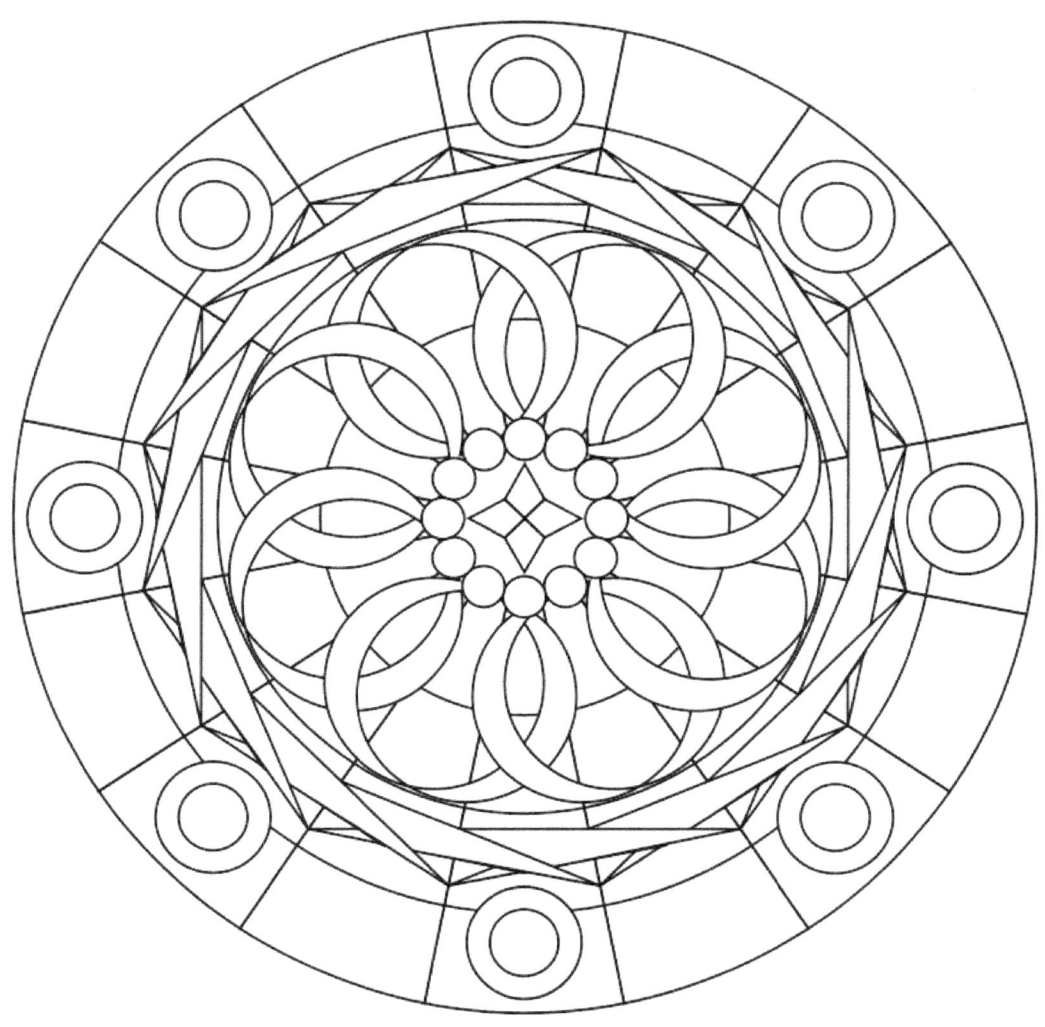

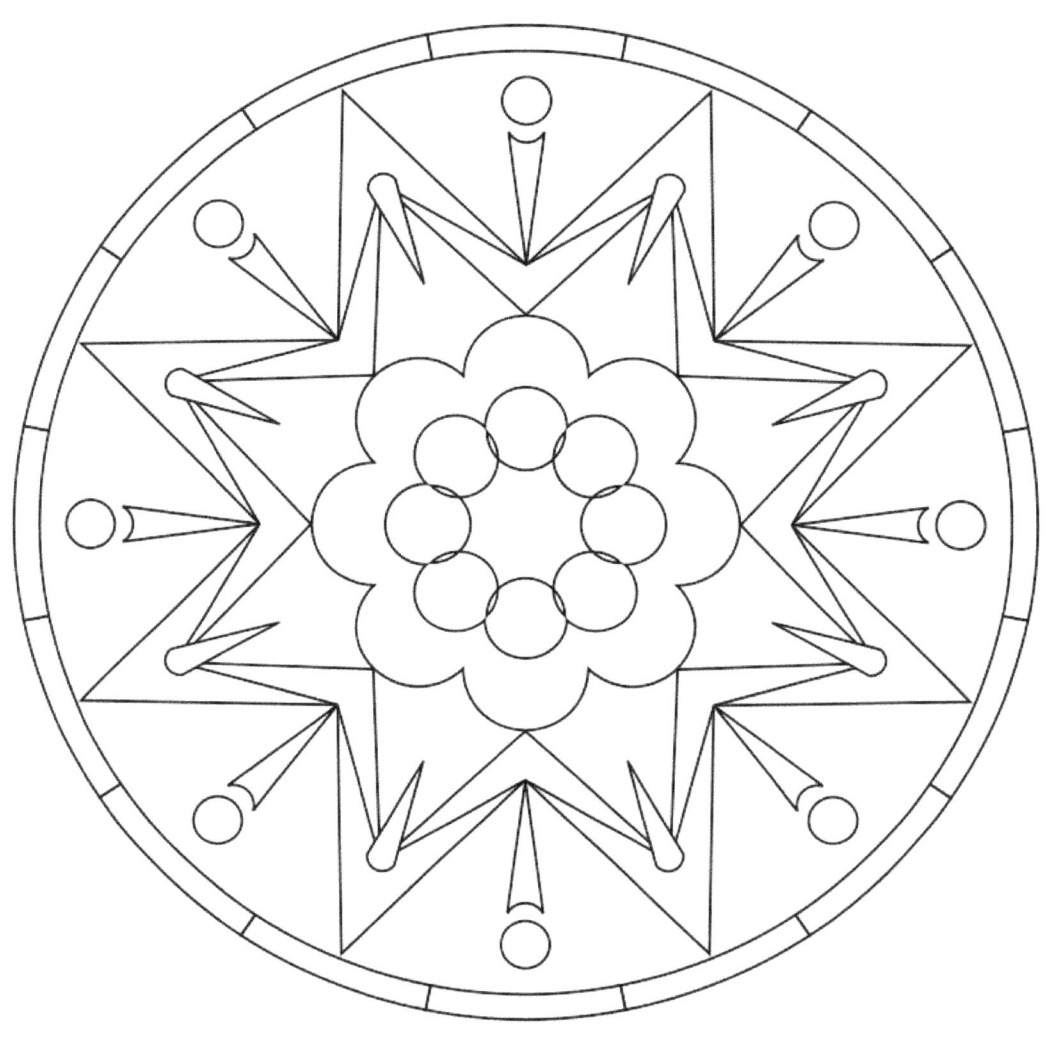

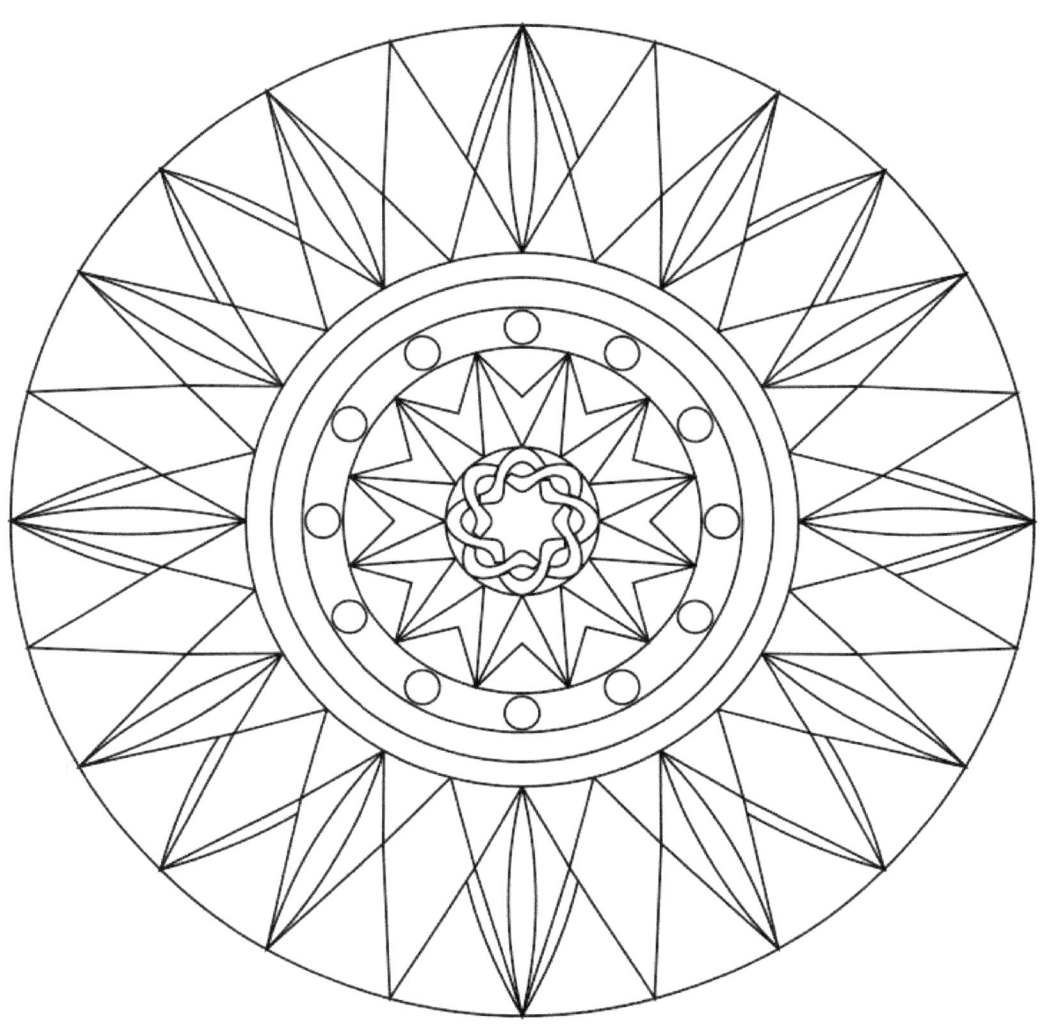

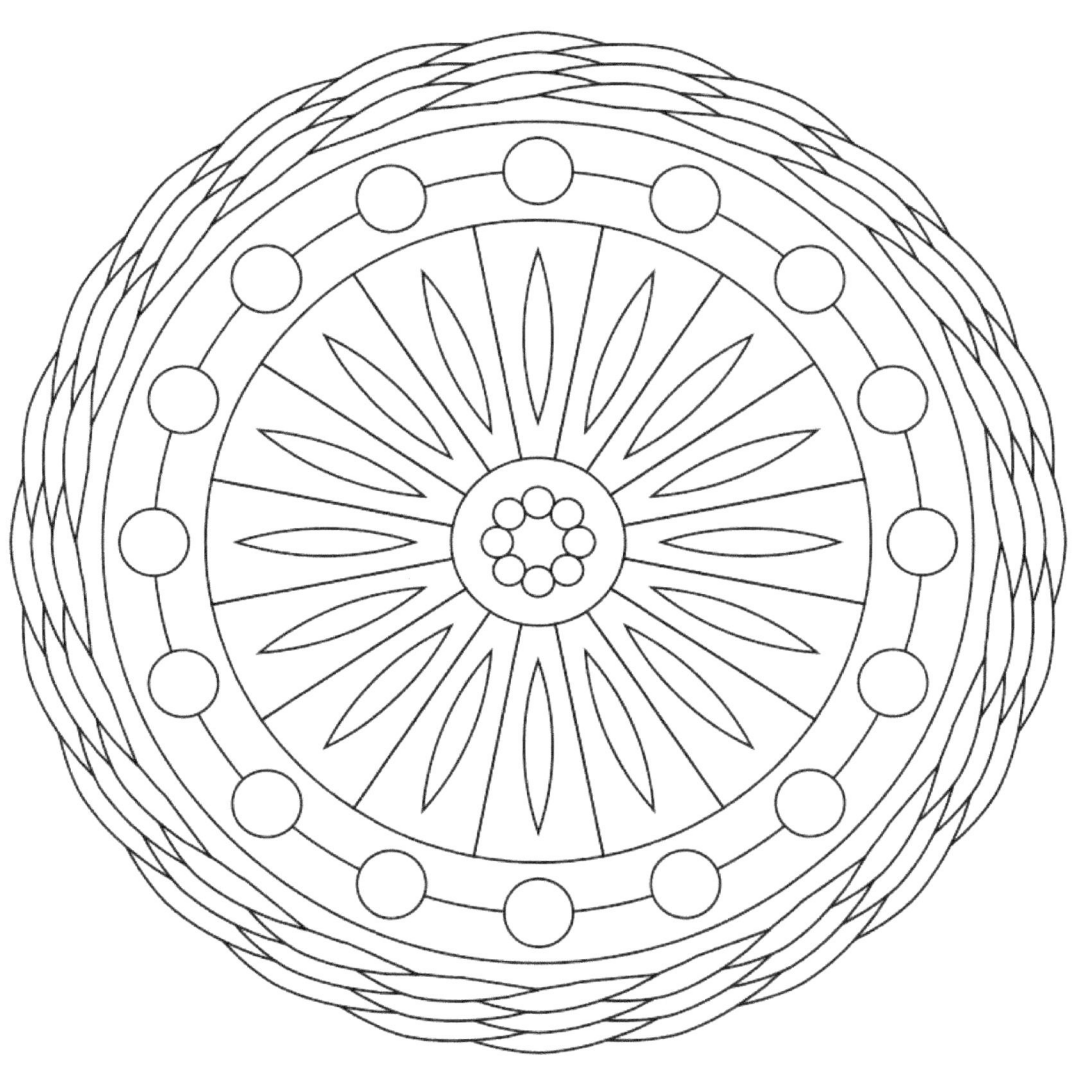

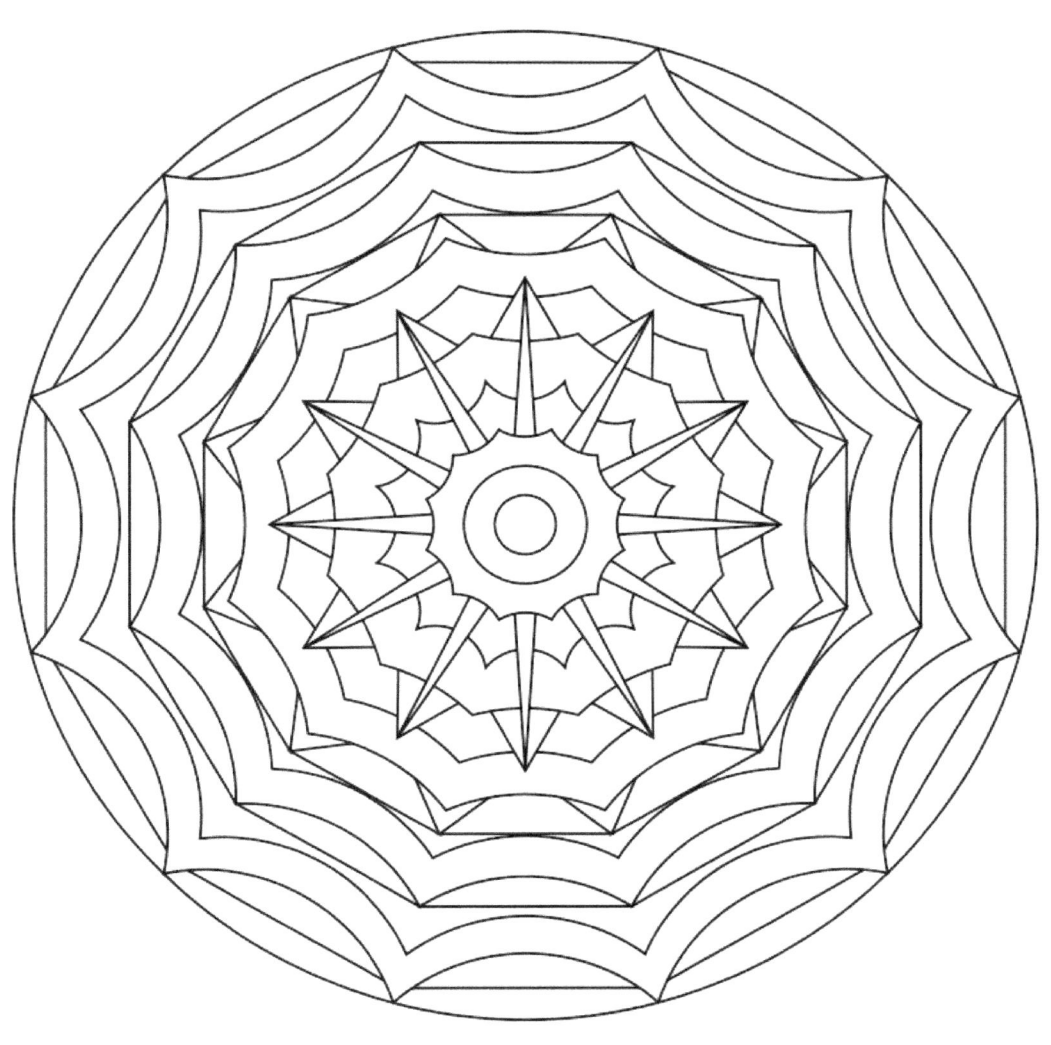

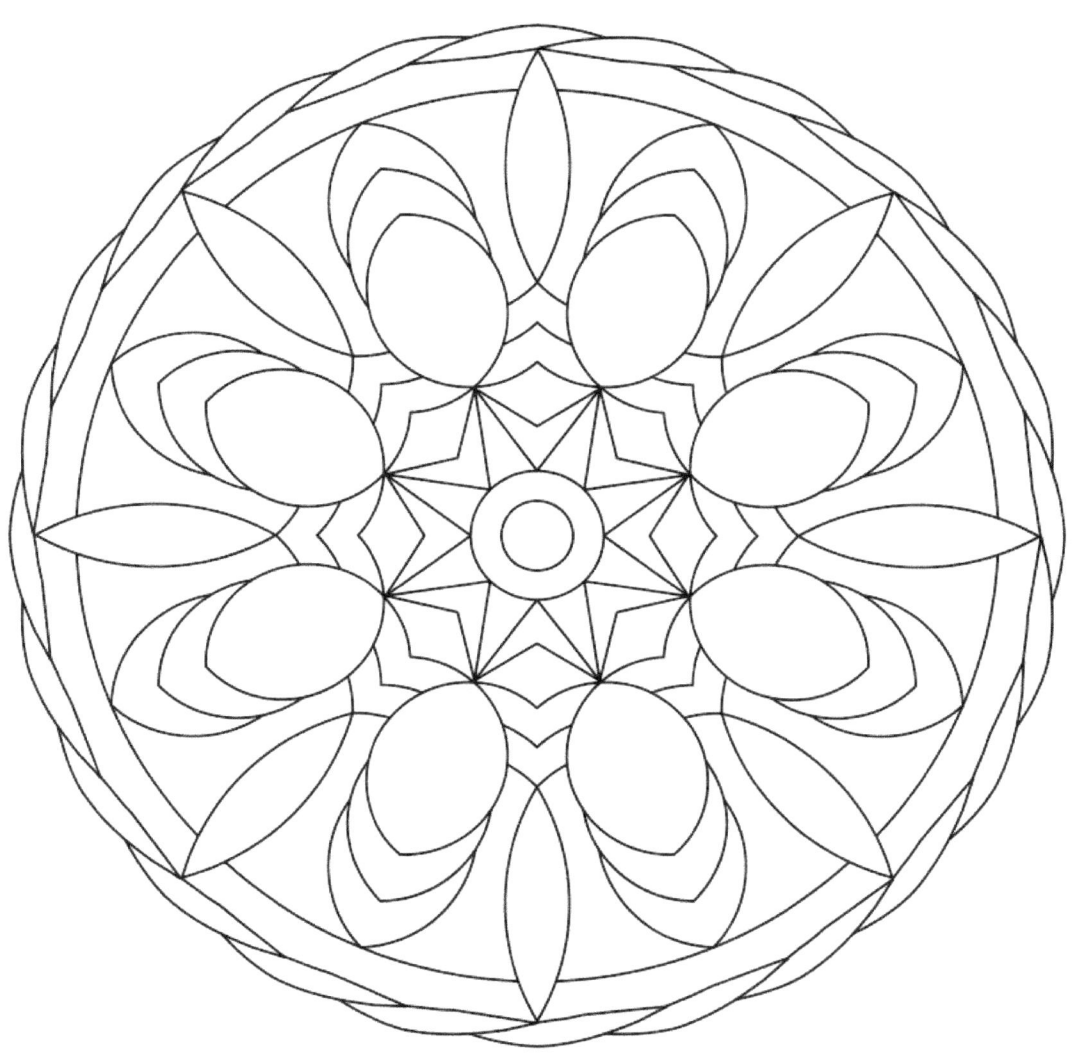

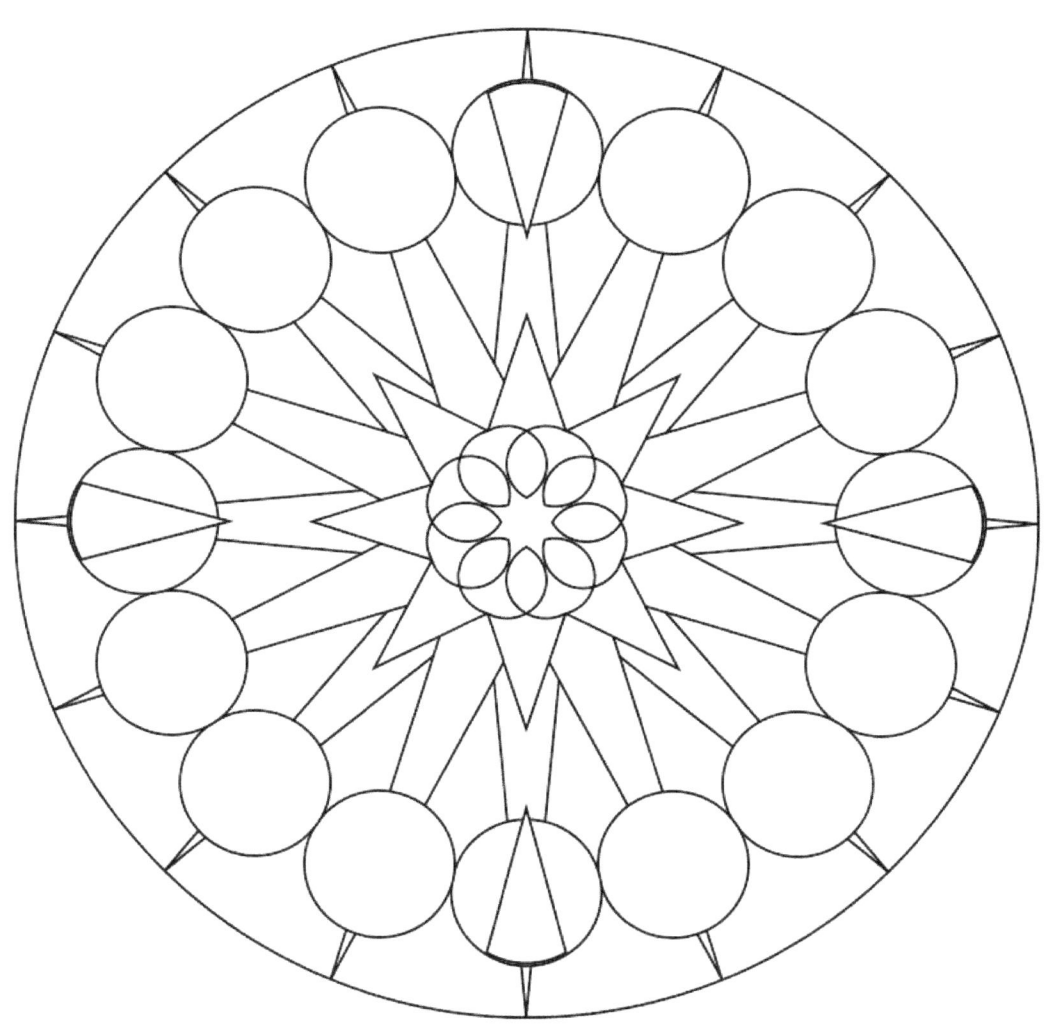

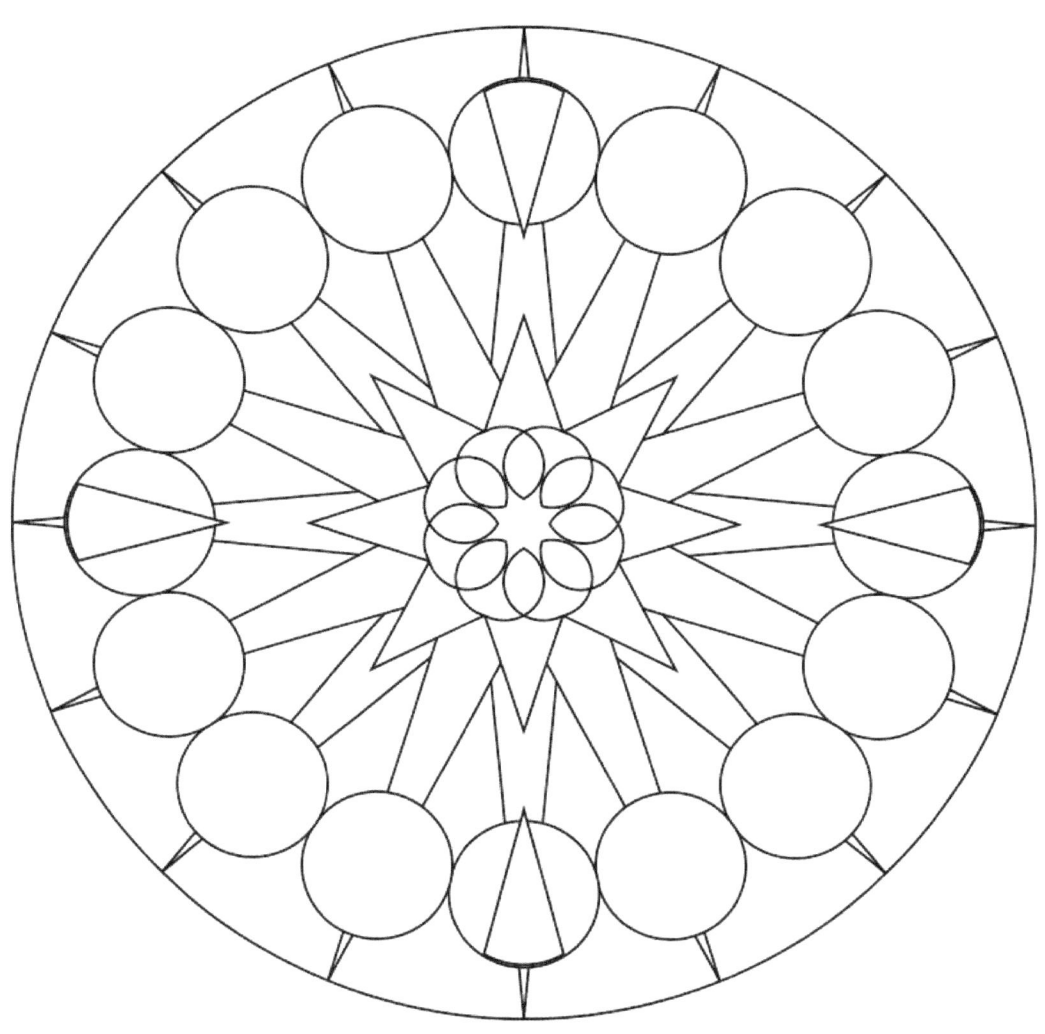

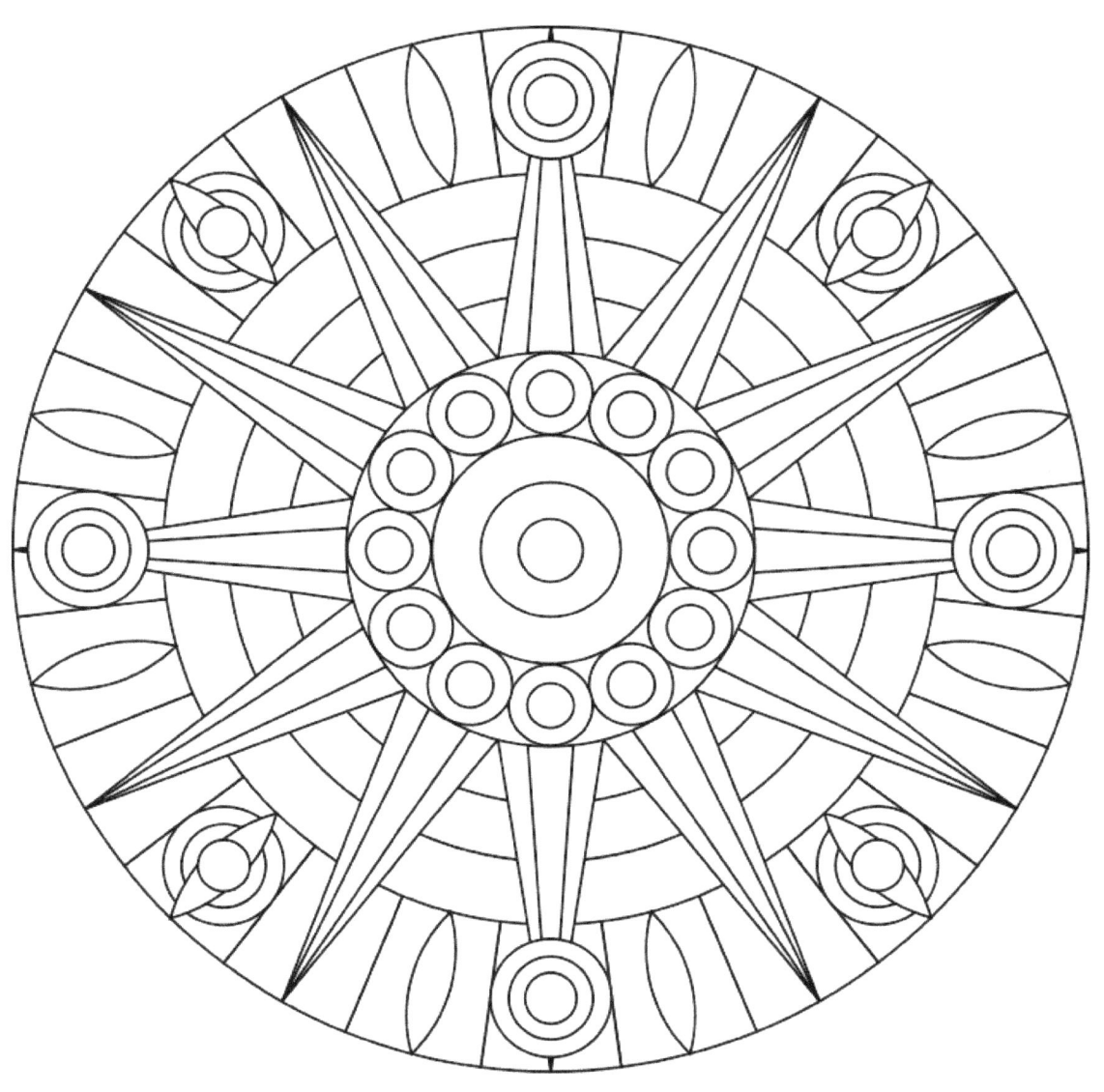

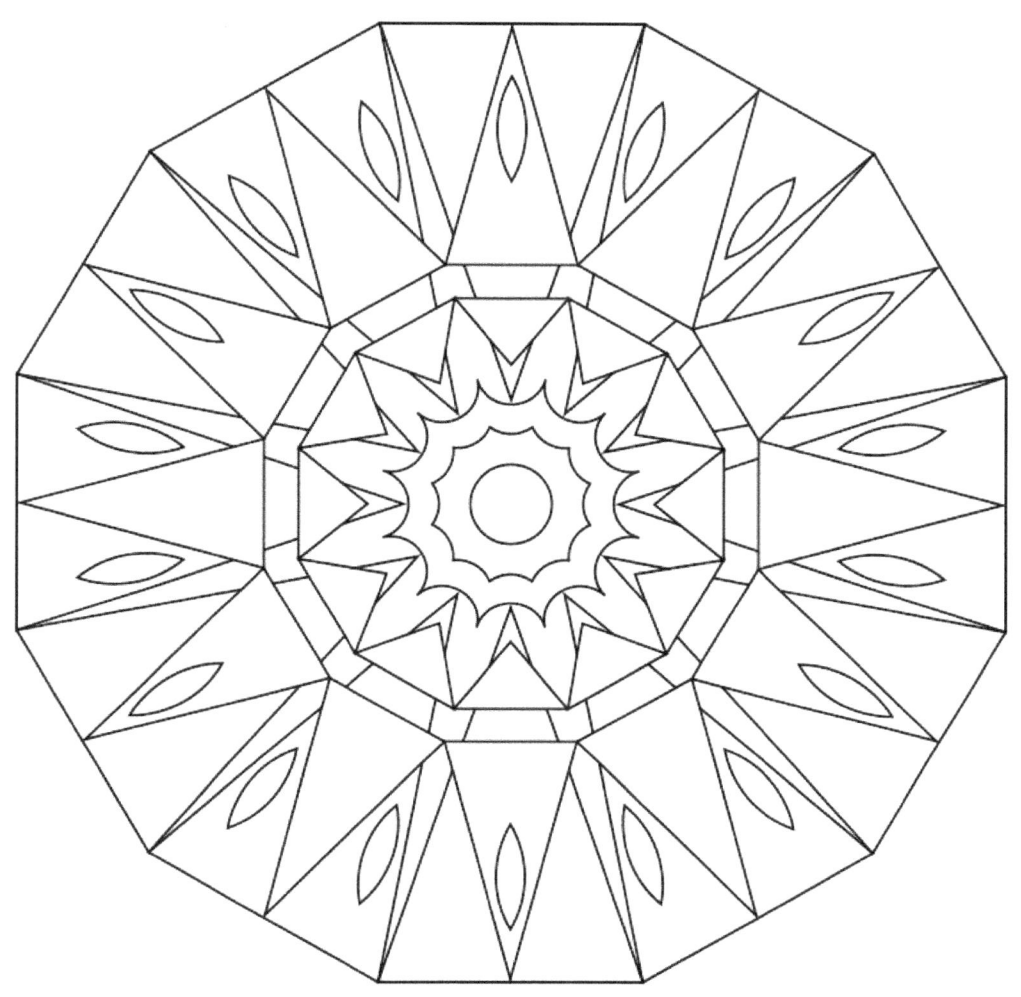

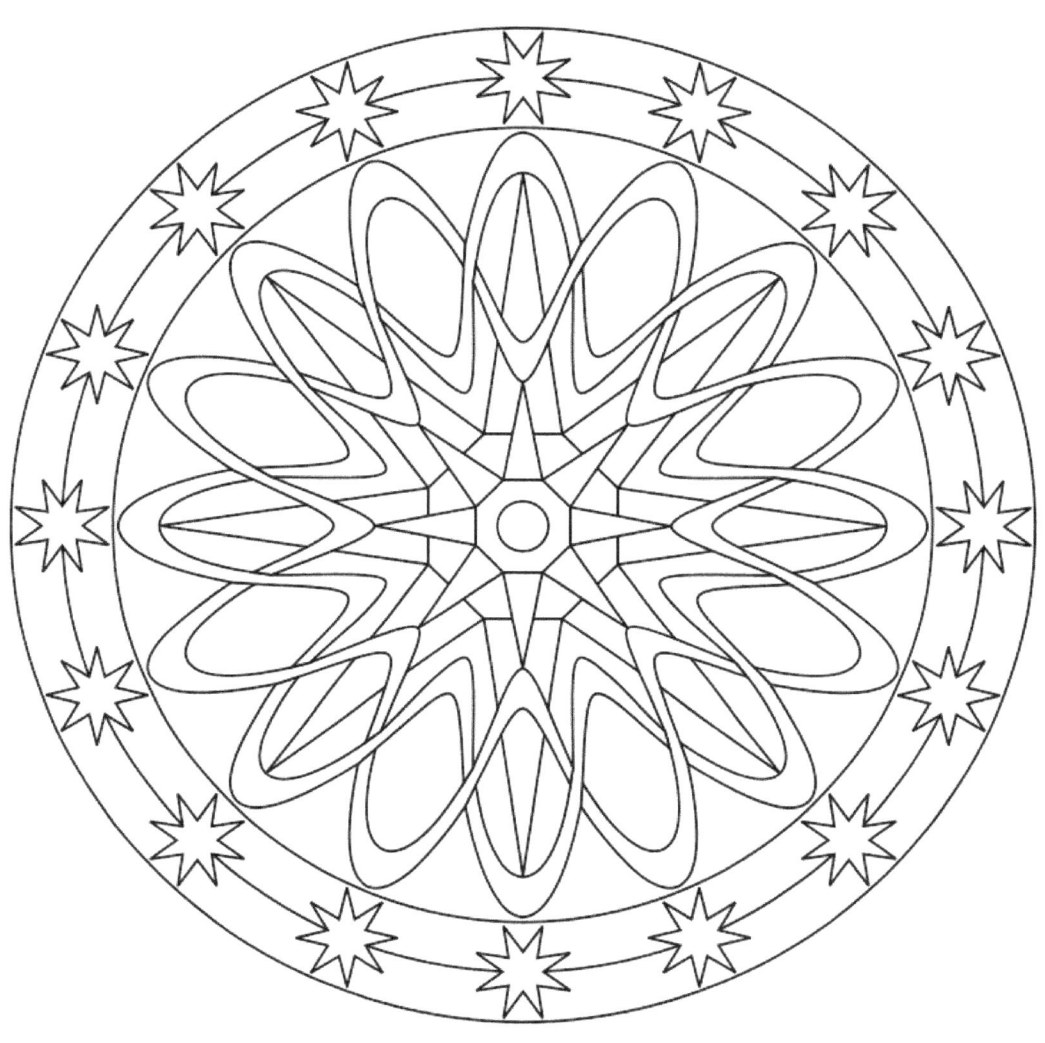

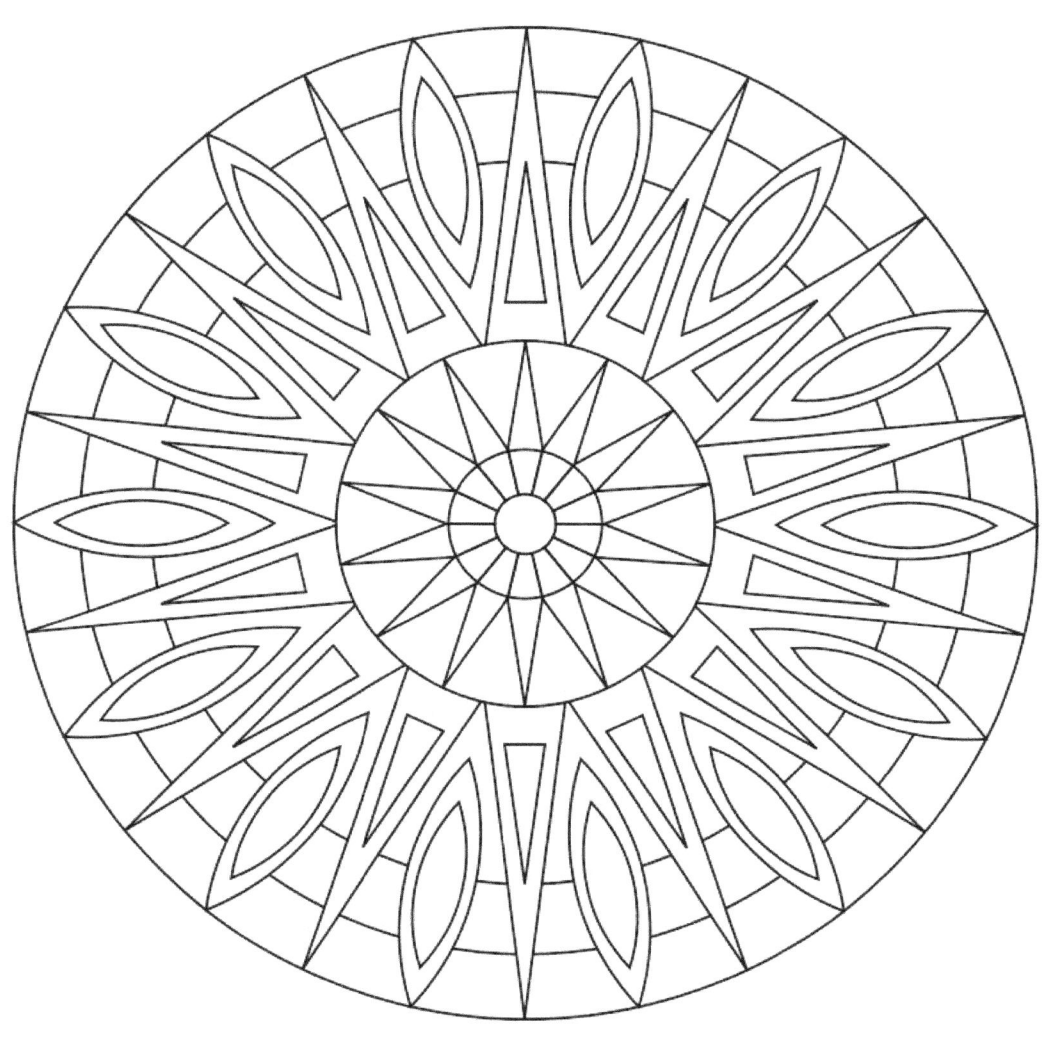

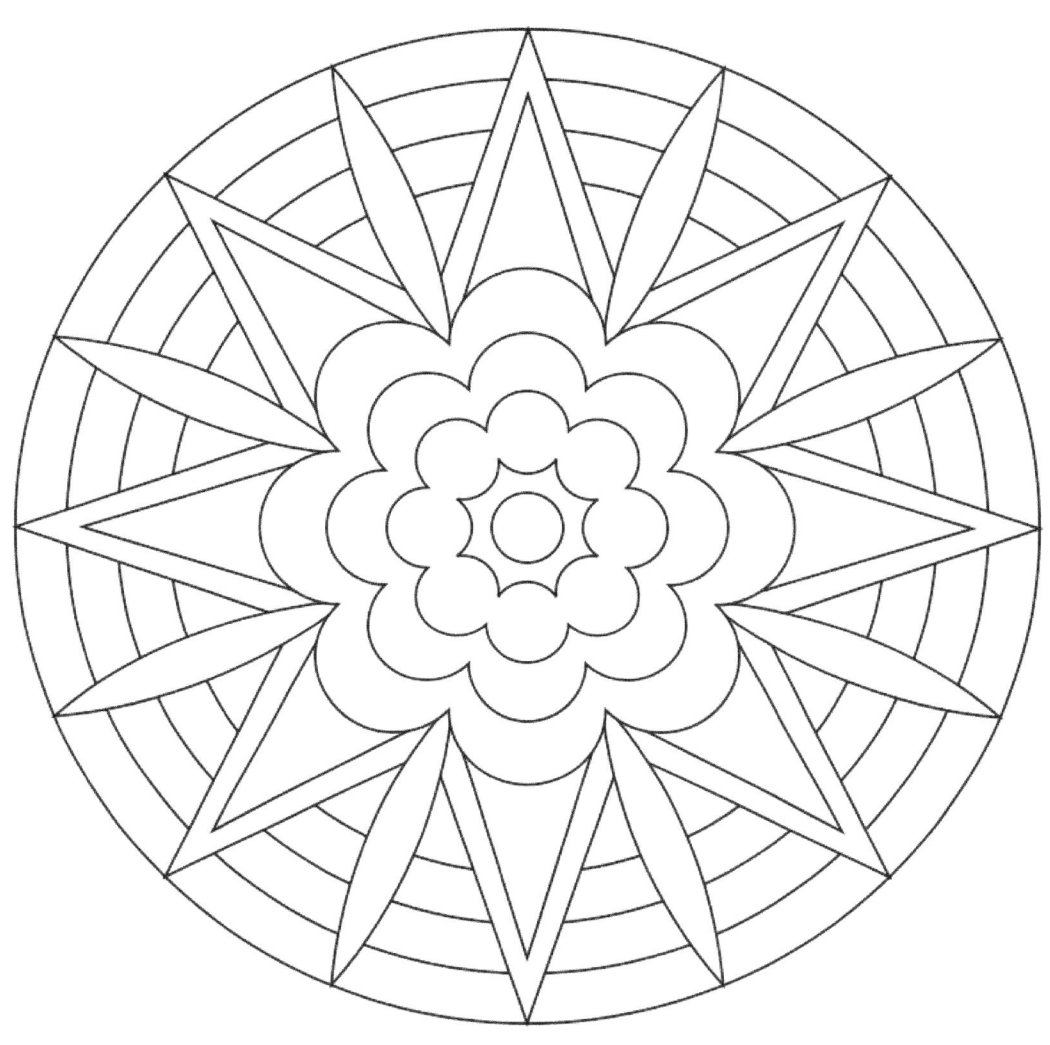

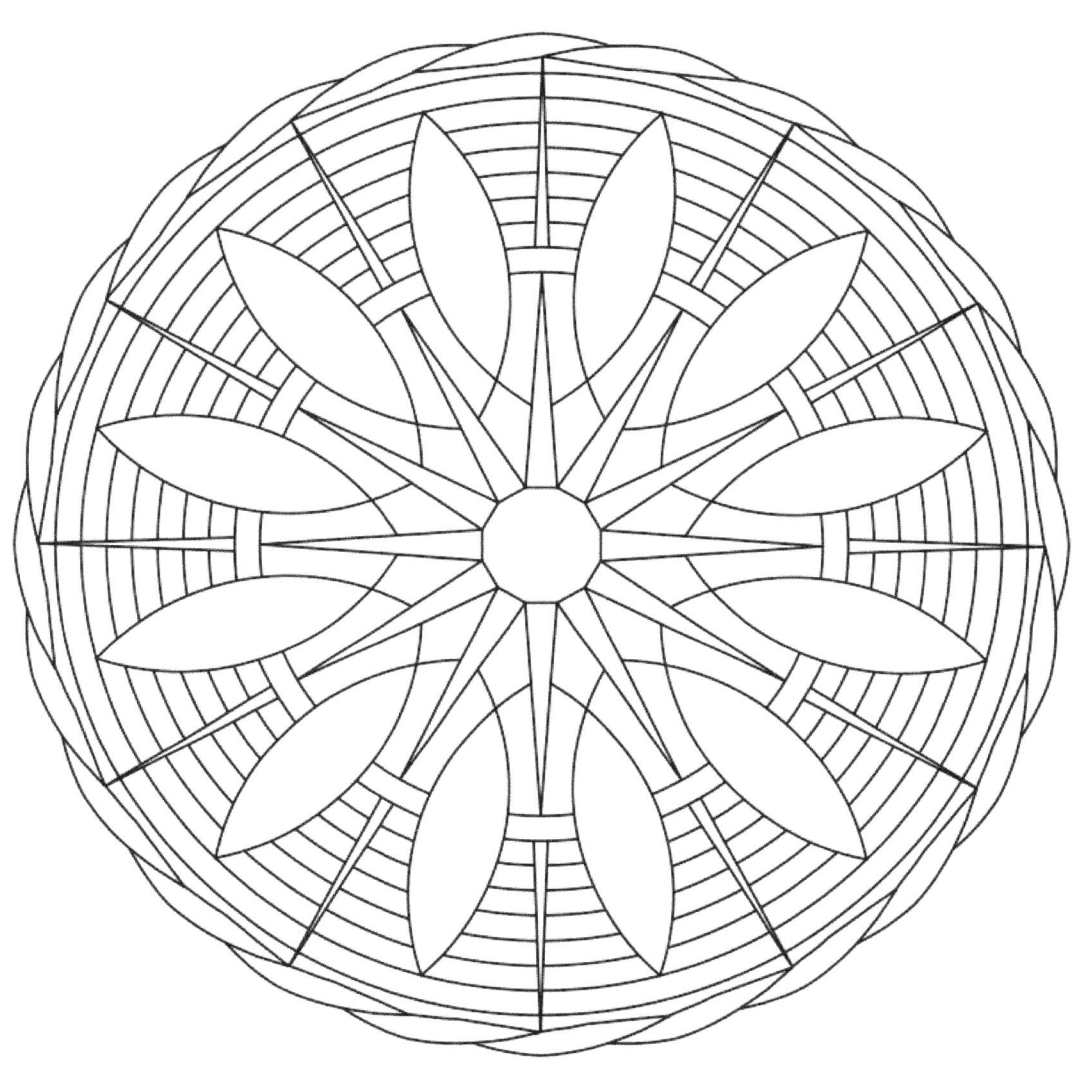

Thank You For Investing In This Book.

Be Connected & Share Your Coloring With us.

Join our Facebook group to share your work
https://www.facebook.com/groups/cosmicmandalas/

Are you on Facebook or other social media??
Sharing your coloring images on Facebook or other social media is fine so long as credit is given to the author at all times.

Here's a fun way to do it.
When sharing your coloring just tag the artist like this : " Artist - Alan Kiddle "
I love to see your work and can't wait to see what you do :-)

Don't forget to join our friendly facebook group for colorists:
https://www.facebook.com/groups/cosmicmandalas/

Questions & Feedback Are Always Welcome:
Email: **cosmicmandalas@gmail.com** or **alan@azenpublishing.com**

See next page for more books available through amazon.
All books also available in PDF for instant download at:
www.azenpublishing.com

MORE BOOKS BY Azen Publishing

To use myBook.to Links :
Just type link as is you don't need to add http or www

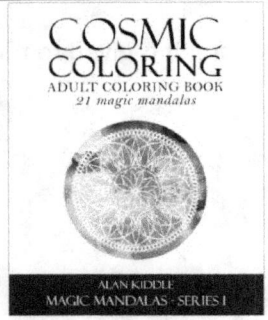

myBook.to/cosmic1

Video Previews
https://youtu.be/ZtappGjVUOE

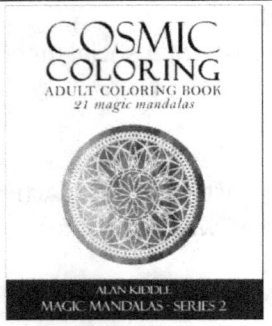

myBook.to/cosmic2

Video Previews
https://youtu.be/EBtApTWqUGQ

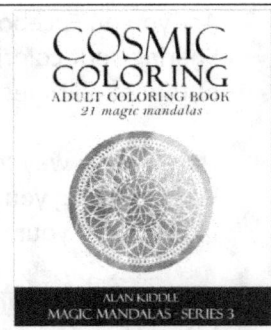

myBook.to/cosmic3

Video Previews
https://youtu.be/OlGb-svDq1M

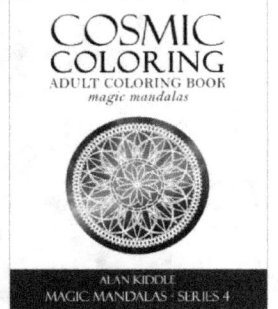

myBook.to/cosmic4

Video Previews
https://youtu.be/9xfr52mnQyk

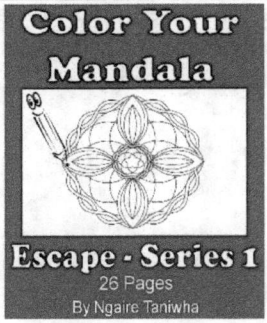

myBook.to/escape1

FaceBook Adult Coloring Group
www.facebook.com/groups/adultscoloringbooks

WEBSITE: **www.azenpublishing.com**

TWITTER : **@azenpublishing**

PINTEREST :
https://www.pinterest.com/azenpublishing/

FACEBOOK COLORING GROUP:
https://www.facebook.com/groups/cosmicmandalas/

FACEBOOK PAGE :
https://www.facebook.com/adultcoloringforfun/

www.ingramcontent.com/pod-product-compliance
Lightning Source LLC
Chambersburg PA
CBHW082031190526
45166CB00017B/2880